Robert
Lawrence
Balzer's
Book of
Wines
&
Spirits

Robert Lawrence Balzer's Book of Wines & Spirits

✛

The Ward Ritchie Press

For E.T-M. and J.A.W.

PREFACE

IN THIS ERA of jet travel, television addiction, and short attention spans in staccato-rhythmed life patterns, books, and even magazines are struggling for survival as dominant communication forms carrying information via the printed word.

Nevertheless, spring and autumn release lists from publishing houses, and crowded bookstores, prove indeed that writers are writing, publishers publishing, and readers reading. But, the grab-span of available time for mass reading is no longer where, what, and how it used to be.

This book is an anthology of brief articles about wines and spirits first published in the PSA In-Flight Magazine. *Flightime*, a monthly periodical aboard this incredibly popular west coast jet airline, is geared for readers during the short flights connecting California's principal cities.

I began writing for *Flightime* with Volume 1, Number 1 in 1965. "Adventures in Wine" was the first volume to emerge from those pages. This is the second. A third, devoted to "The Wines of California," is in preparation.

In this current anthology, our aim is not in the direction of comprehensive, in-depth coverage. Rather, we researched the most topical subjects and included them for your daily use and pleasures. Recipes were added, and often the full original text of an article where magazine space had brought in the inevitable blue pencil cuts. Familiarity does not breed contempt along the wine trail. Such is also the case with the moderate hosting of the domestic bar. Knowing just this much more about each of these chaptered wines and spirits is bound to enrich the link between beverages and friendly hospitality. Such has been our aim.

Our gratitude here goes particularly to PSA Magazine publisher, Jeffrey Butler, for permission to reprint words and pictures from his magazine. Our thanks also to Jurgensen's, Bullock's Santa Ana, Tiffany and Van Cleef & Arpels of Beverly Hills for their generosity in loaning "props" from wines to rubies, used for our photographs accompanying each article-chapter.

And lastly, a special bow to Ward Ritchie, one of America's most distinguished publishers and book designers. His gentle persistence has brought these pages together. Thus, we may all continue the deeper pleasures that books, as books and as beautiful treasures, continue to be, even in this age of non-intellectual and short span diversions.

Robert
Lawrence
Balzer's
Book of
Wines
&
Spirits

The Subtle Art of
WINE TASTING

IN THE DIVINE SCHEME OF THINGS, we are all given the same sensory equipment, but alas, our less than divine condition leaves us with a curious inability to communicate precisely what our senses can discover. What we see, smell, taste, touch, and hear may be a single stimulus, but our interpretation will founder or expand only in relation to previous experience. We enjoy the familiar. We like best, that to which we are accustomed. Preference is seldom objective.

Fine wine is among the most enjoyable products of man's creative genius. Ever since Noah planted the first vineyard, and made wine, it has served to nourish and comfort. Wine-making was already a sophisticated art in the flourishing Roman empire, and far from unappreciated by poets in the Golden Age of Greece. Two thousand years later, we are only two or three decades into an understanding of the quixotic nature of fermentation, allowing us, perhaps, finer, more flowery, fragrant and tasteful wines than have ever been known in the whole round of vintage history. Enologists, through laboratory analysis, are able to fractionate the complex elements which comprise the body and breath of this volatile fluid, diagnose its color, appraise its condition, and predict its future. Viticulturists can hybridize grape species to produce new varieties that can offer the excitement of taste elements in advanced harmony, like the Emerald Riesling. The goal in all of this scientific advancement is beyond the field and laboratory . . . for better wine . . . to enjoy at table.

The riddle of discovering "better wine" is the fun of the wine game. Good wine always leads to another bottle; a good experience prompts the possibility of another one. It's something to talk about. The innocent easily becomes initiated into the by-ways of the connoisseur. On the threshold of each discovery is the wish to share the pleasure—in communication. Wine is a beverage of companionship; it makes good company.

11

Once over the hang-up of foolish ritual, happily today almost totally a thing of the past, most customers are ready to enjoy wine for what it is, not for what someone else says it's supposed to be. The tasting experience, however, *is* expanded, made more meaningful, and even more joyous with increased sensitivity, penetrating the complex nectar that shimmers in the glass like a liquid jewel!

With sensory equipment alert, the *eyes* behold the color; the *nose* detects fragrance and bouquet; the *tongue* and *palatal* chimney discover taste and aroma, simultaneously with an instant *touch*-awareness of body. The impressions are fleeting, and invite repetition.

We can taste only *sweet, sour, salty, bitter,* and *metallic.* The survival area of the brain can unscramble scents with super-computer speed into *spicy, flowery, fruity, resinous, burnt,* or *foul.* The co-existence of plural stimulae simultaneously prolongs the challenge of wine-tasting. But alas, some of the nerve filaments, particularly of scent, fatigue quickly, but fortunately revive with considerable efficiency. You can refresh your palate with nibbles of bread, a thing that happens automatically while you are enjoying wine with food. Assuming your taste-experience has been comprehensive, you are ready to interpret your findings.

Our concern here is not that of the professional enologist, but merely communicating the joy that resides in wine, sharing enthusiasm on a plain-talk level. It abhors the condescension of the memorable Thurber cartoon character who described a wine as "A naïve domestic burgundy without any real breeding, but I think you will be amused with its presumption." As an exercise in increased awareness, it's fun to spin the computer of relevance of the mind's memory-bank for associations. Wines, indeed, do look like rubies, sparkle like diamonds, own the color of gold, sometimes suggest in their fragrance the scent of roses, violets, apples, dried grass, currants, raspberries, sandalwood, tar, or pine; and in taste subtly suggest almonds or spices; and have the touch of velvet, silk, or satin. The cold thrust of reality, however, is sobering to the poetic muse, for if you were to walk into a room where a precious bottle of a rare vintage Chateau Haut-Brion had been dropped and broken, you would certainly not describe what you would be smelling as wild violets and raspberries! You'd say "Wine!"

There are only five classes of wine: *Red Table Wines,* which will include Rosé; *White Table Wines; Sparkling Wines; Appetizer Wines,* which include Dry Sherry and aromatized wines like Vermouth; and *Dessert Wines,* such as Cream Sherry, Port, Muscatel, and Madeira. As subjects for comparison, each should be considered in its own category. Purists will argue that comparisons should only be made further within geographical regions, that it is an error to taste a wine of France against one of California. To expect them to be similar and fault them on difference is gross error, indeed, but finding relative associated merits is a delightful pastime. The Cabernet Sauvignon grape has definite varietal characteristics, no matter whether its roots grow in Bordeaux calcareous clay, or Napa Valley loam. Once you've become accustomed to the taste of one Cabernet Sauvignon from one vineyard, by drinking it regularly, another example from another vineyard will provide an instant awareness of challenging difference. Similarly, the Rhineland of Germany offers a dazzling, and sometimes confusing, confrontation of white wines all produced from one grape species: the White Riesling. The vines in each separate little plot, harvested separately, vinted separately, produce individual wines, but again, with familial resemblance.

In the span of 24 hours recently, I visited two northern California wineries occupying polar differences in their approach to winemaking. They have equally opposing goals, which they pursue with equal intensity, toward high quality wine. One winery is among the largest in California; the other, one of the smallest, small to the point of being almost primitive. The winemaker in the small winery ages his white wine in wood, allowing it to take on both color, and a hint of wood in the taste. It is bottled, corked, and laid away to acquire some bottle-age. One of the goals of the large winery is to obtain the maximum identification with the delicate taste of the grape. After a cool fermentation, the wine is *briefly* aged in wood, and then held in glass-lined metal to rest before bottling, so that its pale brilliance will have no detectable alien influence. The enologist is working for a non-cork closure, so that not even the minimal cork-contact will violate his goal of simon-pure better wine.

We are conditioned in our taste-acceptance by our own individual histories. Today's market shows a trend toward table wines with an ameliorating, fractional hint of sweetness. Often it's barely detectable, but makes the wine softer, less harsh, and at once pleasing to generations that have grown up on soft drinks, candy bars, and an unconscious rejection of even slight bitterness. *Dry,* erroneously equated with *bitterness,* is incorrectly dubbed *sour.* In the most sophisticated circles of wine drinking, the alien taste of wood and cork (presuming healthy wood and cork) have traditional acceptance. But among the higher echelons of professional enologists, the trend of preference is towards dry wines with an ultimately non-woody perfection, coming from capture of the pure miracle of the grape's virtue as wine.

A vocabulary of wine appreciation is easy to build once you've analyzed the job to be done by your eyes, nose, mouth and palatal chimney. Wines can be great or small, robust or thin, impressive, charming, powerful, fleshy, balanced, clean, gentle, crisp, sprightly, engaging—all words you might use to describe a friend, acquaintance, or new-found love. In this there is seldom hesitation, nor need there be in the equally subtle appreciation of wine.

Notes

CHAMPAGNE
The Wine of Natural Grandeur

WHEN I WAS VERY YOUNG, moving into my teens in the Prohibition era, Champagne was legendary. The word had an aura of its own, bespeaking elegance and an almost unattainable social perfection abounding in grace. Like a Rolls Royce, it was costly, too, setting it apart from all the other wines. One could read about it, and a few privileged souls probably tasted it from time to time on festive occasions when a few bottles would appear furtively from illegal private hordes. The only place it was common was in literature describing the most enviable of society's continental *purlieux*. This only added to the prejudice being engraved upon my adolescent consciousness. Champagne and all sparkling wines had an empyreal aspect. This was not diminished in any way when, as an awed college freshman, I was taken to a posh San Francisco speak-easy where, with the ultimate in *savoir faire*, the host's request, "You may pour the wine now," brought a resounding report of a popping cork, and the liquid, foaming rubies of Sparkling Burgundy bubbled into tall, stemmed crystal glasses. In the words of Daisy Ashford, it was a most "sumpshous" occasion!

If the name Daisy Ashford does not mean anything to you, one of life's merry treasures is still yours to discover. Sir James Barrie (*The Little Minister, The Admirable Crichton, What Every Woman Knows, Peter Pan*) assures us that Daisy Ashford's pencil-written novel of the high life in London at the turn of the century, in "The Young Visiters," is the unaided effort in fiction of an authoress of nine years. Barrie's Preface to "The Young Visiters" explains the naïve spelling, grammar, and punctuation, but only marvels at the *"idears"* which passed through the life and times of heroine *Ethel Monticue* and her *Alfred Salteena*, "an elderly man of 42." Unquestionably, Daisy Ashford only knew of Champagne as I did, vicariously, but it belonged most definitely to *"socierty"* and *"Aristockracy"* which our young nine-year-old novelist explains, is composed of *"peaple (sic) who have got something funny in their family and who want to be less mere if you can comprehend."*

Champagne remains among the best ways I know of letting life become any kind of "mere." Champagne is the least *mere* of all wines, but the whole purpose of this chapter is to let you in on the real truth about sparkling wines. They are indeed most elegant, but there's no reason to be in awe of them, as I was, leaving them, as did Daisy Ashford, to the *"most sumshious . . . levie at Buckingham palace . . ."* where folk *"strole round and eat ices and champaigne and that kind of thing . . . with men of a noble nature dressed like the earl in satin knickerboccers etc and with ladies of every hue with long trains and jewels by the dozen"* . . . where *"on a golden chair was seated the prince of Wales in a lovely ermine cloak and a small but costly crown."* Champagne certainly belongs in such circles, but it tastes just as good creaming out of chilled bottles in any of the living rooms of the nearest suburbia.

Champagne is expensive only because of those bubbles. Ever since the 17th century days of Dom Perignon who started using cork to stopper the bottles of new wine in the antique French province of La Champagne, the imprisoned carbon dioxide gas of voluntary or, as at first, involuntary secondary fermentation in the bottle, captured those drinkable "stars." But that same secondary fermentation produces, as we all well know, a most unattractive sediment, which has to be gotten rid of somehow. The old way, the classic *Methode Champenoise*, still in use in the Dom Perignon caves of Moet & Chandon, in the subterranean carved chalk cellar-caves of the best of all houses of Reims and Epernay: Ayala, Bollinger, Charles Heidsieck, Clicquot, Heidsieck-Monopole, Krug, Laurent-Perrier, Mercier, Mumm, Perrier-Jouet, Piper-Heidsieck, Pommery, Roederer, Ruinart, Taittinger, has each separate bottle shaken nose-down in riddling racks hundreds of times until, months and months later, after the *years* of horizontal storage before riddling and clarifying, the sediment is expelled and the brilliant sparkling wine ready for its *liqueur d'expedition*, or final dosage. This latter will determine the minimal amount of rock-sugar and Cognac syrup used to change the taste from *Sec*, to *Extra Dry*, to *Brut*, or the driest of all, with literally no sweeting, *Natural*. *Extra Dry* and its drier complement, *Brut*, are the most popular types.

Several aristocratic "Blanc de Blancs" made of selected berries from selected bunches of Pinot Chardonnay, as in the *epluchage* of that most elegant Comte de Champagne bottling of vintage Taittinger, are dry, dry, dry. The 1961 vintage is now eleven years old (Champagne allegedly lasts 17 years, but can, under ideal cellar conditions, last longer. I tasted a bottle of Mumm's Cordon Rouge 1904 vintage in the cellar of Baron von Mumm almost fifty years after the wine was bottled, and it still had a thread of bubbles. But that was most unusual). Bottlings of Chardonnay champagnes are always expensive, not only because of the labor of production in hand-sorting of grapes, but the time *and* the cost of that Chardonnay *cuvée,* or basic blend.

Not all the elegant Champagne and sparkling wine comes from Europe, or even France. Italy sends us its delightful Asti Spumante, and Lacrima Cristi Spumante. From the banks of the Rhine, Germany provides a bottle-fermented charmer—Henkell Trocken. Sometime try making your own "Kalte Ente" or *Cold Duck,* by pouring a bottle of Henkell Trocken over a peeled lemon spiral dangling in a pitcher containing a bottle of your choice Moselle which, too, has been kissed by the lemon spiral. Then dance. Paul Masson Vineyards, of Saratoga and the famous Champagne Cellars, calls their version of Cold Duck, *Very Cold Duck* because it's very special, one of the few bottle-fermented blends of Champagne and Sparkling Burgundy the market affords. The rest are bulk-process. All the American bottlings of this curious wine-of-fashion called "Cold Duck" are sweet beyond belief! But popular! Daisy Ashford would call them "scrumshious!"

There's no reason to wait for a ship-launching, birthday, wedding, or anniversary ball to think in champagne terms. One of the delightful things about our American wine heritage, and especially the California portion, is the excellence of the premium sparkling wines. Paul Masson astounded Parisians in the year 1900 by capturing an award for his California Champagne. It's still, seventy years and some several hundred gold medals later, a match for many of the finest from La Champagne. On his recent visit here, Claude Taittinger, of that noble house, had equally kind words for our premium sparkling white wines which, unlike Madame Bollinger, he admits, are generically "Champagne"—"California Champagne." This would include the Blanc de Blanc of Almaden, the Natural of Korbel, the Brut of Paul Masson, and the Blanc de Blancs of Schramsberg. Less expensive, and almost as good, are the Charmat bulk-process California Champagnes of the Christian

Brothers and Llords & Elwood. New York has its Gold Seal, Great Western and Taylor New York Champagnes which are fine for New Yorkers and their eastern neighbors, but if you're out West, California wines have no competition except that from France and Germany.

Almaden has a "sleeper" with a dba label called "Le Domaine" California Champagne which, the last time I looked, was selling for about $3 per fifth. It has a plastic cork which explodes like a bullet once released from its wire hood, so be wary; but the wine is delightful, pearling with elegance.

I'm over my awe of champagne. I can even spell it with a lower case "c", and take the left-over bottle into the kitchen to cook with it. The last experiment was so successful, I had to *buy* a small bottle to re-create the same experience.

No greater compliment can be paid to a few friendly callers who've announced an intention of dropping by at an appointed time than popping the corks of one or two elegant bottles of the finest champagne: a Taittinger or Roederer Crystal-bottle, or one of our premium California Champagnes. It comes on with its own magic.

For those special "friendly callers" here's another compliment to pay them—a most special lemon pie, with champagne to lighten the pastry crust.

Fresh Lemon Meringue Pie

The Pastry:

1½ cups all purpose flour	1 teaspoon salt
½ cup shortening	¼ cup champagne (or white wine)
	¼ cup grated or flaked coconut

Sift flour with salt. Cut in half of the shortening with a pastry blender until it resembles corn meal. Then add remaining shortening, blending to the size of small peas. Moisten portions of the mix with the wine, with two forks pushing the whole into a ball. Chill briefly. Dust the ball of pastry-dough with flour, then roll out between two sheets of wax paper, or roll out on a lightly floured board or pastry cloth. Fit into a 9-inch pie pan, fluting the edges. Press coconut into bottom. Prick with a floured fork. Bake in a very hot oven 450° for 10-12 minutes or until tawny. Remove to wire rack to cool.

The Filling:

4 egg yolks, slightly beaten with	5 tablespoons cornstarch
1/3 cup lemon juice (fresh lemons only)	1/4 teaspoon salt
2 tablespoons grated lemon peel (2 lemons)	1 1/2 cups boiling water
1 cup sugar	2 tablespoons butter or margarine

Mix egg yolks and lemon juice and set aside. In a saucepan, thoroughly mix sugar, cornstarch, salt. Gradually stir in boiling water. Bring to a boil over medium heat. Stirring constantly, over reduced heat, cook clear filling 2 minutes as it thickens. Stir in egg-lemon mixture *gradually*, slowly. Bring back to boiling point for one minute. Remove from heat. Add butter and grated lemon peel. Pour hot filling into cooled pastry shell. Top with meringue. No need to cool before topping with meringue.

The Meringue:

4 egg whites	9 tablespoons sugar
1/4 teaspoon cream of tartar	1/2 teaspoon vanilla
1/4 teaspoon salt	1/2 teaspoon lemon juice

Beat egg whites with salt until frothy, add cream of tartar. Beat in sugar, one tablespoon at a time, until meringue is stiff and glossy. Add flavorings and beat again. Pile onto pie filling, spreading thoroughly to the edges. Bake in a moderate oven for 15 minutes or until golden brown. Allow to cool, *thoroughly*. Serves 8.

With champagne, this lemon pie will give delicious evidence that you don't need to be "rubbed up in Socierty ways"—you've already arrived! You've taken the awe, but not the grandeur, out of champagne.

Here are some more ways to elevate celebration moments with champagne:

BLACK VELVET: This is a 'come-in-the-kitchen-and-watch' marvel if made in the traditional manner. Hold 6 ounces of cold Guinness stout in one hand and 6 ounces (1 split) cold champagne in the other and pour them into the glass together. Otherwise pour the stout first and then slowly pour in the champagne, being careful not to stir. Don't talk about this one, just drink, before it flattens.

CHAMPAGNE COCKTAIL: Please use a traditional 6-8 ounce wine glass and not one of those saucer-shaped misfits some call a champagne glass. Ugh! Pour about 6 ounces cold champagne into the glass and twist a strip of orange peel over it so as to let the oil breathe, and drop the peel in. Add 1 teaspoon of brandy, very slowly so that it floats on top of the liquid.

CHAMPAGNE PUNCH: There are probably a dozen variations of this around, but this is basic for about 20 servings. In a punch bowl place 6 lumps of sugar, 1 cup good cognac and sprinkle with bitters. At serving time add 3 bottles of *cold* champagne (nothing wrong with California, and the price will not lighten your purse too much). You may add ice in a block, of course, but some special shape is always fun.

MOSELLE PUNCH: Place 6 oranges, very thinly sliced, and 1 cup fine sugar in a bowl. Pour 1 fifth Moselle or other dry white wine over the fruit and walk away for an hour or more. In a large bowl put a block of ice and pour this mixture over it. Add another bottle of the wine and 3 bottles of chilled champagne. This will make about 25 servings.

CHAMPAGNE CUP: To serve four begin with a cup of in-season fruits: peach, lemon, orange slices, strawberries, cucumber peel and so on. Add 4 ounces each brandy, Benedictine and maraschino liqueur. Put into a 2 quart pitcher or bowl and refrigerate for an hour or longer. Just before serving pour in 1 bottle of cold champagne and about 6 ounces fresh spring water over a dozen ice cubes or a small block of ice. Add a cherry to each glass and stir before serving.

NOTE: In all of the punch-type recipes it is crucial that the bowl, glass or pitcher be thoroughly chilled. Also, fresh spring water, or Perrier water is the sign of a true punch and not the carbonated beverage often used.

Additional Recipes

A Renaissance for the Image of
ITALIAN WINES

IN QUICK ASSOCIATION, "Italian Wines" evoke an imagery totally disconnected from the elegance of their proper heritage. Checkered tablecloths, and candles dribbling wax down the necks of straw-wrapped flasks once filled with rough young Chianti precede any thoughts of the dazzling splendour surrounding the birthplace of this antique wine. But this same Tuscan wine was poured at the tables of the Medicis, in whose Florentine kitchens *haute cuisine* had its origins, later exported to France. Then and now, Chianti had its common and uncommon place. There was young wine, and aged vintages, humble table wine and treasured pourings.

The provender of Italian gastronomy is according to the purse commanding the table, unlimited in delicious and classic possibilities. Thumb the 800-odd pages of Luigi Carnacina's "Great Italian Cooking," or drool your way through Ada Boni's "Italian Regional Cooking." If there's a gene of the scholar in you that hankers after knowing how the Caesars and Toga'd amphitryons of Imperial Rome wined and dined, spend some hours among the pages and paragraphs of "Apicius," probably the first cookery book of defined civilization, notably Italian, and inspirational these nineteen hundred years later.

Benvenuto Cellini, Leonardo da Vinci, Michelangelo, Andrea del Sarto, and Bronzino, along with Ghiberti, Donatello, Luca della Robbia, and Verrocchio provided an aura of grandeur surrounding the Florentine dominion which still survives to illuminate the creative corners of the living marketplace. The contemporary thrust of *fiorentinata*, a word that has been synonymous with exquisite taste, fine craftsmanship, and compelling originality is not confined to the silks of Emilio Pucci, the leathergoods of Gucci, nor the modern counterparts of Cellini in silver, gold, and hand-wrought jewelry. It extends into the fields and cellars of wineries with an aesthetic tradition. It is visibly emerging on limited amounts of wine, far beyond the daily

25

consumption bulk, in pedigreed bottlings carrying a signet of government regulation.

D.O.C. or the full phrase, *Denominazione di Origine Controllata*, incorporated into the label legends of Italian wines separates the finest produce of the vineyards from the ordinary. But more than that is necessary to find those bottles of wine that can become an aesthetic experience. You must look for them with knowing eyes.

Discrimination is still the crest-jewel of the cultured citizen. His mind scans the field and makes the taste-rewarding decision out of knowledge. This separates the boys from the men, and amateur from the professional, the glutton from the connoisseur. It makes wine-buying a stimulating adventure of assured pleasure, rather than a random gamble with frequent disappointment. The late André L. Simon succinctly defined the territory: "A connoisseur is one who knows and loves that which is good, beautiful, uncommon, interesting, everything that is the best of its kind, and above all, genuine. To become a connoisseur, one must be keen and one must be trained."

A few brief paragraphs cannot presume to be that education to which M. Simon refers, but they can serve to highlight the possibilities open to the shrewd shopper, widen his horizons of search, and unveil some exciting menu-building possibilities beyond that humble Chianti in the straw-wrapped *fiasco*.

The whole boot of Italy is full of wine. It's made in every province and principal island. From the warm south to the alp-touching north, grapes produce every variety of wine with distinctly regional differences. Just as the old Florentine Dominion of Tuscany is Chianti-country, Piedmont is Barolo and Barbaresco country along the Nebbiolo vine trail. Lambrusco country is certainly more famed for its fizzy purple wine than its provincial geographical handle, Emilia-Romagna. Veneto really brings Venice and all things Venetian to mind, which includes not only the fragile, ethereally wrought glasses, but the wines that are poured into them from Soave, Bardolino, and Valpolicella. Sicily? Marsala, of course, but there's more—a table wine called Corvo, well worth a few more words as we narrow our focus on specific bottlings of assured value, such as the red and white wines from vines growing on the crater-slopes of Mount Aetna from the Baron de Villegrande.

There's no attempt here to be comprehensive in scope. Five regions can provide a sampling to qualify our thesis of a new look at the Italian wine scene. Happily, too, it won't cost an arm and a leg to drink the proof of the argument!

Tuscany: Sixty percent of the wine exported from Italy is Chianti. Of that shipped in *fiaschi*, the straw-wrapped bottles, Cappelli is an outstanding bargain at $2.19, and another seldom-heard name, Ancilli bearing a 1964 vintage, at $2.49 represents the Chianti Classico heartland with distinction. But if you're looking for red wine of more complex richness and distinction, not merely a pasta companion, the finest wines of Tuscany (Chianti) come in Claret-style bottles. Nozzole 1962 Chianti Classico has the delicacy of a fine Bordeaux, albeit full-textured. From the Villa Antinori, there are *Riserva* bottlings of older wine for rich enjoyable sipping, with nibbles of cheese; as a distinguished *aperitif*, as well as dinner service with steaks, chops, and roasts. The same is true of the Melini Riserva 1964.

For several centuries, the wine-growers of the Chianti Classico region have marked their vintages with a protective seal, red-edged, with a black rooster on a golden field. Look for it. Be on the look-out too, for a red wine called Brunello di Montalcino.

Piedmont: Barolo is the biggest red wine of Italy, and often its best. Deep in character, pressed from Nebbiolo grapes, it becomes velvet rich only with age, beyond five years, and it can live more than twenty under proper storage. A heady 14 per cent alcohol by volume, it invariably requires opening at least two hours in advance of serving, and will even then expand its virtues after it has been poured. A glass of Barolo from a well-aged bottle can eloquently tell even the novice what the fascination of fine wine is all about. The perfume is complex, with a whole *pot-pourri* of scents, reminiscent of dried rose petals, marjoram, sandalwood, and tar. Try the Barolo of Renato Ratti from the hills of La Morra, called Abbazia Dell'Annunziata, or that distinguished bottling of Bersano. You may have to be patient. The 1964 vintage is still too young for the full potential to be realized, but if you buy it now, you'll be ahead on the price when the wine is truly mature.

Veneto: The delectable, fragrant white Soave, which is a superb accompaniment for abalone, crab or sole, in chilled and generous glasses is most reliably excellent from Bertani, Bolla, Lamberti and

Santi. Here, youth is in its favor. Don't worry about specific vintages in Italian wines. Like California, most years are good, and dates merely serve as identification for specific lots.

From the Valpolicella hills surrounding Verona, the legendary city of Romeo and Juliet, comes an extraordinary wine called *Recioto* made from the "ears" of the bunched grapes, those which stick out and get the most sun, and develop the most sugar. It's a complex and rich red wine, sweet when made sparkling, or *spumante*, and hauntingly dry when fermented from loft-dried grapes, and called Amarone. The Bertani, Lamberti, Santi, or Bolla Amarone is an adventure in taste, but only for the true winelover who savors somnolent dryness. Big, heady—it goes with cheese—*after* the roast!

Sicily: When the Turks invaded Sicily in the 16th century, they named the picturesque seaport *Marsah Allah*, "God's Harbor." Two centuries later, a Britisher, John Woodhouse, who supplied Lord Nelson's fleet with wines, copied the traditions of Spain and Portugal in adding brandy to the local wine, and the world came to have the sweet elixir of the grape called Marsala! But the volcanic soil of the island has other vineyards on the slopes which produce dry table wines of sound traditional merit, notably Corvo. Those vintages from the vineyards of the Duca di Salaparuta, estate-bottled at Casteldaccia in Palermo are an interesting variation for the winebuff to taste, at no more than the cost of a good California Cabernet, or about $2.50. The white Corvo is green-gold, sprightly, clean. The red is a beautiful ruby, truly *sapore*, a flowery nose, perhaps a little thin, but the Sicilian *cepages*, of Catanese and Perricone grapes provide an interesting adventure that invites repetition. Italy gives "Oscars" for its wines, and the red Corvo-Salaparuta won the golden Mercury Award in 1968. The label is handsome, the wine a great bargain.

The "renaissance" affecting Italian wines halts abruptly at the doors of the wine rialto—the marketplace. Historically, Italian wines are sold primarily in Italian restaurants. Our purpose here is to throw the spotlight on bottles that belong in your own cellar, at home, to be poured at your own table. Do you know the taste of Est!Est!!Est!!!, Lacrima Christi, Lambrusco, Orvieto, Greco di Tufo, Verdicchio? Fresh strawberries and Asti Spumante are certain to be a dessert combination of memorable consequence for the host who is having the fun of adventuring among wines.

Once upon a time, only emperors could command wines for their tables from far off vineyards. Today, they're no further than your nearest supermarket or wineshop, available glamor for menu-building without spending a fortune.

Golden Wine of the Magyars
TOKAJ

ONE OF THE MOST MAGNIFICENT wines in the world today is also, curiously, one of the least known in popular trade—the luscious Hungarian Tokaji-Aszu, created by the princes of Transylvania in the 17th century.

The history of the lush golden wine is no less dramatic than its taste. It begins, triumphantly, with the bequest of Carpathian territory by the Emperor Probus (276-282 A.D.) as reward to his soldiers for Imperial Roman victories. They carried the civilization of the Eternal City into the provinces, including the refined art of winemaking. And so it happened, when the horse-mounted Magyars swept over the plains of Hungary, they found vines growing on the slopes of the volcanic Hegyalja mountains. Contemptuous of farming, they turned the care of vineyards over to their prisoners, whole colonies of Germanic tribes. But the legendary wine rose from a later wave of civilization, when the ultimately canonized Magyar statesman Stephen I, led his pagan people into the Christian fold of the Roman order. Italian advisers were imported and, under their influence, the antique Roman vineyards along the River Bodrog, northeast of Budapest, enjoyed an early renaissance in the year 997.

As a crossroad territory for the caravan traders bringing silk and spices back from the East, the language and cultures of Hungary took on exotic touches of the Orient, including a new grape vine known as the *Froment*. Their word for wine, *bor*, derived from a Turkish root, instead of the Sanskrit *vena*, which birthed the Latin *Vinum* and French *vin*.

Strife came to Hungary with yet another invasion in the 16th century, and prolonged conquest by the armies of the Turkish Sultan Suleiman. For all these years, the law of the Prophet Mahomed prevailed, prohibiting wine drinking, but Christian natives still tended the vines and, it may be presumed, sold and consumed the wine. The Grand Chamberlain of the restored Hungarian Emperor, Ferdinand, imported a colony of German winegrowers. Their highly specialized skills produced a magical wine that was made from over-ripes grapes touched by *edelfaule*, the *Botrytis cinera* "noble rot" fungus, which shrivels grapes into richly sweet raisins-on-the-vine *(trockenbeerenauslese)*. It produced such a golden wine from the *Froment* grapes (today called *Furmint*), that rumor soon spread that the wine of the Tokai village contained gold! A German naturalist claimed he had found "gold seeds" in Tokai grapes. A Swiss alchemist, the notorious Paracelsus, came to investigate. He was set upon by Tartar bandits, but managed to reach Tokai Hegyalja and its vineyards. Raiding Turks and Habsburg armies had long before forced the natives to hide their wine in deep mountain caves, where they were protected and preserved. Paracelsus' memoirs record no gold discovery, but give a possible explanation of the wonder of the wine: "the vegetation here amalgamates with the earth's minerals and the sun's rays in this district in such a way that a golden thread traverses the vines and their roots and then penetrates the rocks below."

Hungarian Prince Ferenc II Rakoczy did the wine of Tokaj its most lasting service of fame when he sent bottles of the exceptional golden wine to the Sun King of France, Louis XIV, who found it so extraordinary he had it placed on all the court menus as "The King of Wines, the Wine of Kings."

For the rest of its history, *Tokaji-Aszu* the rich wine of the village of Tokaj belonging to the crown, never lacked royal patronage. Emperor Franz Josef of Austria elected it as the annual birthday gift for Queen Victoria, with a dozen bottles for each year of her life. The last gesture; on her 81st birthday, in 1900, saw 972 bottles of the rare elixir dispatched to Balmoral Castle.

The restorative powers of *Tokaji-Aszu* and *Tokaji-Esczencia* in actual therapeutic value have some illustrious case histories. For one, when Pope Leo XIII was dying, a courier from Vienna to Rome brought him bottles of the wine for eight weeks, and according to the late wine merchant of London, Charles Walter Berry, "nothing passed his Holiness' lips for this length of time save this wine, and it kept him alive at his tremendous age." Rich in minerals from the volcanic soil of its origin, easily assimilated, it has brought systemic assistance to the ailing and fatigued with remarkable results.

There are about 5000 acres in all that comprise the Tokaji-Hegyalja vineyards strung along the 17-mile chain of hills descending through northeastern Hungary. But it is not the volcanic soil, nor the *Furmint* grape that spells the wonder of *Tokaji-Aszu*. It is the peculiar, indigenous method of its making that accounts for its elegance.

Furmint grapes of the Tokaj vineyards are picked late. Those touched by the *edelfaule* are gathered separately and placed in baskets or wooden hods called *puttonyos*. *Aszu* is a foot-trampled mash made from the finest *edelfaule*, or *trockenbeerenauslese* grapes. Its consistency is correct when a handful of the mash, squeezed in the hand, sends the sweet paste oozing out between the fingers, leaving only seeds inside the fist. This is *Aszu* dough. One *puttonyos* will hold 30 pounds of *Aszu*, and serves as a measure for the next step in making the wine. To the regular must of crushed *Furmint* grapes, from one to six *puttonyos* of *Aszu* dough is added per *gonc*—35-gallon cask. The resulting combination must of a 5-*puttonyos Aszu* wine will be as high as 30 per cent sugar. In the cool mountain caves of Tokaj, after a primary 12- to 48-hour fermentation, the workers trample it again, through hand-woven cloth. The wine will then go on fermenting slowly, to a heady, sweet strength of impervious lasting power. Airspace is always left in the *gonc*, which may account for the aromatic bouquet, not unlike the fragrance of fresh pumpernickel bread.

Tokaji-Eszencia, a regal essence, is seldom available for export today. Its vinification goes on, however, bowing to ancient Roman traditions allowing only the weight of grapes alone to extract the nectars for winemaking. Untrampled *Aszu* grapes are collected and placed in a vat, in the bottom of which is a small opening, fitted with a goose quill spout. Only the drops of juice that drip through this tiny aperture, as much as 50 per cent sugar, will become wine, in a fermentation that may last several years. As one of the most immortal wines on earth, it invariably can outlive its vintner.

Tokaji-Aszu is available today in America. The 5-*puttonyos* golden wine sells for approximately $5.95 in pint bottles. As final punctuation to a dinner for discriminating guests, *Tokaji-Aszu* will bring taste memories that will endure for a lifetime. It is sweet, but not cloying; serve it only slightly chilled.

The Rich Taste of
PORT

LOOKING TOWARD the ski-slopes of Heavenly Valley at Lake Tahoe is a handsome chalet called *The Christiana*, its modest signboard legend announcing its restaurant, cocktail lounge and lodging, and almost inconspicuously, Tahoe Institute. What goes on within under the latter name is a mystery to most local folk; guests-participants and directors are drawn from the outside ranks of the new science born of psychological counseling—*sensitivity training*. The workshop staff and directors are nationally prominent professionals devoting weeks and week-ends on programs uniting re-creation and recreation, swinging profoundly, so its guests may become alert, alive, dynamically in touch with family, self, and nature. Tahoe is a natural for this dramatic indulgence, in all seasons. There's obvious skiing in winter, boating, swimming, fishing and golf in summer, and five minutes from *The Christiana* and Heavenly Valley, the Nevada side, with headline entertainment, gambling casinos with all the neon razzle-dazzle of Las Vegas.

Turning-on to taste was one of Tahoe Institute's week-ends, which involved group appreciation of superlative wines and foods, with full awareness.

Before you turn off, or sit in the scorner's seat, allow a few more words. What may seem kooky might touch the common quick, where we're all enjoined by our built-in survival equipment, the five senses: sight, hearing, taste, smell, and touch. There's much talk about a "sixth sense" by metaphysicians, but psychologists by-pass this one for a more physical reality of a muscular sense compounded with the nervous system related to touch, and a seventh sense, visceral, relating to the instinctive reactions of the nervous system. All seven, if you will, are dulled by the assaults of modern metropolitan living, robbing even the anxious of a proper share of good living. Deodorants, air-fresheners, filters, preservatives, and an extravagant range of refining processing keep us apart from all but what our society deems desirable, or enjoyable. Our processed foods have become so dull, we need an additive to make them taste like what they're supposed to be! The experience of a tree-ripe peach, apricot, or pear is almost unknown. There are thousands of children in our country who've never tasted a fresh orange. Moving into the realm of luxury, to consider the rich taste of Port Wine, and its combination with cheese, this glorious experience is often robbed of its full potential because the selections are made without discrimination arising from knowledge. Conclusively, the palatal experience is reduced if the awareness is not awakened to what *might* be. Wine is more than wet, more than alcohol and sugar, more than red, white, pink, or sparkling, more than fermented grape juice. It is a compound address to all the senses except hearing, so clink your glasses, and make it complete.

The rich taste of Port can climax a dinner, extending conviviality long past dessert or coffee, with fruit and cheese and good talk. But only when it's a worthy wine, not just a cheap bottle from the nearest supermarket. Men invariably choose cheese with applied discrimination. Port, for some reason, too often gets less attention. To some, "Port" is "Port" and thereby hangs a tale. Not so, by a long shot!

The word "Port" derives from the Portuguese city of Oporto, where the winding river of the Douro region meets the sea, where the casks of wine made in the upper regions are aged and blended, and bottled for shipment all over the world. The British solidified the Port wine industry in Portugal in the 17th century, foisting the brandy-laced red wine of Portugal upon the public when the customary red wines of Bordeaux were prohibited by the fortunes of war and politics. Public resistance was loud and eloquent at first, but little by little, the addition of brandy to young, new, red wine became an art. Age, either in wood or bottle, softened the wine to something elegant, fragrant, beautiful to the eye, and warming to the heart and mind. "Port" became a generic term. It was understood all over the world. "Port" wine was made in every wine-growing country of the world, in varying degrees of excellence. As you might expect, Portuguese wine growers have long been unhappy about the appropriation of their proper name by producers in other countries. It took them a long time to act, but now they've done it. The original is now legally protected, and to be called *"Porto."* "Porto" labels are already appearing in the market, and soon, *all* Portuguese Port will identify itself as "Porto."

Federal label regulations in the United States still properly insist upon the true place of origin in direct conjunction with all generic titles, so we shall continue to have California Port Wine, and even England will have its Australian Port Wine and South African Port!

In Colonial America, it was a gentleman's preoccupation to choose his Madeira wines with pride comparable to his choice of women or horse-flesh. It revealed him openly to his peers when it was served. Port has played a similar role at the British table, the decanter moving counter-clockwise around the mahogany. Vintage Port always required decanting, because it acquired a heavy crust of sediment lying binned in bottles as many as 20 years or more before being served. The perfume and taste of such wine is an experience never to be forgotten, and alas, today, seldom encountered. But the market offers splendid Porto and excellent California Port, worthy of time taken in selection.

Briefly, how is this wine made? In Portugal, some 2500 different grape varieties are grown and used in making the wine, the best of which are the Tinta varieties, the Touriga, and one called Souzao, which gives deep color and fruity taste. Color extraction from the skins, the cap of the must, occurs during fermentation. Before all the sugar has been converted, brandy is added to arrest fermentation, and the resulting wine has stabilized sweetness. As it ages, in wood or glass, it loses color; it goes from rich ruby to bronzed tawny. Careful attention preserves the natural glycerines which contribute a richness of texture, visible in running rivulets, streaming down the sides of the glass when it is swirled or tilted. These are the "tears" of the wine, or its "legs" or "cathedral windows" arching back into the bowl.

Inferior port wine is sometimes sweetened, or flavored with grape concentrate. California regulations prohibit the use of any sweetening agent other than grape concentrate. California regulations do not specify grape varieties for Port, nor qualitatively define the fortifying brandy. Needless to say, the broad range of possibility in the making of port wine anywhere in the world, will produce an equally broad range of wines.

Criteria of judgment? Beyond price, which is the quickest separation of the good from the bad, it is logical to assume that Porto from Portugal will cost more than Port from California. It is not necessarily true that a cheap Porto will be better than a comparably priced California Port. The premium port wines of California are not inexpensive.

Port wines from both Portugal and California vary in degrees of sweetness. The cheaper wines are usually sweeter; sugar masquerades a wine's more obvious flaws of delicate acid-balance and natural fruitiness. Ruby Ports generally have a freshness and sprightliness, while Tawny Ports will have a soft languor and bronzed elegance from greater age. California varietal ports, of Tinta or Souzao grapes, as made by Ficklin, Almaden, Christian Brothers, Paul Masson and others, have a unique taste-character of notable complexity and refinement, worthy of lingering enjoyment.

Port wine obviously appeals, in sensory address, to sight, for its glorious color, to smell, for its complex bouquet, to taste, for its sweetness; but its *rich taste* sensation rides on its appeal to *touch!* This is *mouth-feel*, one of the least mentioned, and most important aspects to the journey of taste-awareness. If you've watched the last few minutes of each television session of the Galloping Gourmet, Graham Kerr, you'll understand how this is done. Or, you may remember the memorable eating scenes from "Tom Jones"! The mouth is touching food and drink, prolonging the sensory pleasure. Inside the mouth, is mouth-feel. Only prudish Victorians, who feared the world of the senses, called this enojyment vulgar. "Vulgar" simply means "common" and so it describes us all, where we live with our senses.

Once upon a time, in my career as a restaurateur, the chef brought me a sauce to taste. I reacted by saying I felt it was not quite right; it needed something. In five minutes, he was back with it to taste again. "Perfect"! I said, "What did you add?" Nothing except cornstarch, he explained, to thicken it slightly, so that its perfection could linger longer on my palate to relate its complexity more opulently. This is the role of the natural glycerins in Port. This is part of their richness.

The rich taste of port wine with cheese becomes an eloquent experience only if all the senses are fully aware. A week-end seminar at Tahoe brought a few guests who were startled to learn what they'd been missing. Have a glass of port. It may taste better now!

Recipes for the Englishman's invention—Port? Or course! Wine translates its flavors to all kinds of delectable edibles and potables. The richness of Port is not easily lost.

38

Fresh Peaches Baked in Port
(serves 6)

6 whole ripe Elberta Freestone Peaches
1 cup Port Wine
1 cup sugar

1 lemon—both strained juice, and rind
Fresh-grated Nutmeg
1 ounce Cointreau

Plunge whole peaches, individually, momentarily in boiling water, to remove peel carefully with paring knife. Combine remaining ingredients, stirring over low heat to blend. Place peaches in a baking dish, and pour syrup over them. Cover. Bake in 400° oven, basting occasionally, until peaches are soft. Approximately 45 minutes or slightly longer. Chill. Serve with Almond Macaroons.

PORT MILK PUNCH: Fill the shaker with cracked ice and add 3 ounces port wine, ½ pint milk and 1 teaspoon powdered sugar. Shake well and strain into tall glass; grate nutmeg on top.

NEGUS: Into a hot whiskey glass add 2 ounces port and ½ lump sugar. Fill with hot water and stir. Grate nutmeg on top.

FLIP: Rich, but so delicious! Combine 1 egg, 1½ ounces port, 1 teaspoon powdered sugar and 2 teaspoons sweet cream (optional). Shake well with cracked ice and strain into chilled glass.

COCKTAIL: Straight up or on the rocks this one will save on the medicine bills. Stir together 2¼ ounces port with ½ teaspoon brandy.

WINE'S FOR FUN

WINELOVERS are a divided camp. Riding the dangerous edge of generalization, one can loosely split the party, as with music-lovers, into two groups, the serious long-hairs and the funky sparklers who enjoy! There is also a sober category of catholic overtones, *catholic* in the sense of accepting the *whole* concept, of wine or music, for the potential enjoyment therein, making no edgy distinction about any particular camp.

In a past issue of *Wines & Vines*, the highly esteemed trade journal of the wine industry, veteran editor-publisher Irving H. Marcus showed his editorial teeth with good humor in reaction to a correspondent who had written with displeasure about the crowded tasting rooms of California's North Coast wineries, pining after the days "where he could taste at leisure" without "the wrong people" to "spoil his pleasure in winery touring." Editor Marcus wrote, "Wine, I believe, has something for all. For the connoisseur and for the neophyte; for the rich and for the not-so-rich; for the few and for the many—and the more the merrier, I say." To which I say "Amen"!

Editor Marcus' correspondent, he indicated, came from the professional ranks of a California university, making his intolerant attitude all the more regrettable. "Maybe," Marcus concluded, "what bothers Van der Ryn (the correspondent) on his winery rounds is the fact that these others aren't taking wine tasting seriously enough. They're so casual. They talk, joke, laugh. Perhaps even worse in Van der Ryn's eyes is the fact that they seem to be having a hell of a good time, seem to be finding tasting *fun*. Imagine"!

Ever since I first put my nose into a wine glass a long time ago, a matter of decades, I've been enchanted with the whole idea of this beautiful nectar called *wine*! The fascination has never left me, and there are still whole worlds of tasting fun ahead, for this is the realm, the sensory realm of inexact subjectivity. There are students of music who listen to a symphony with the analytical mind of a mathematician, following the score without hearing the music. There are traditionalists and technicians among winelovers, too, who become so in-

41

volved in rites and ceremonies, presumptive standards and yesterday's vintages they cannot appreciate the delicious cup of now. For all such self-defeating souls we have only true sympathy that their pastures of pleasure are so strictly fenced.

Wine is for fun! Don't let anybody tell you otherwise. If you like it, drink it! If you don't, leave it alone.

However, it might be an idea to investigate the reasons underlying some of the larger truths; like why red wine tastes better if it's not chilled, and why a dry white wine goes better with the fish. Time and tasting will prove the truths of such old ideas, but in the meanwhile, if you like Boone's Farm Apple Wine because it's a groove with those bubbles, enjoy! Spritzig!

Wine—from apples?

Quickly, before traditionalists can lose their long-haired cool, allow me to quote the unimpeachable *Encyclopaedia Britannica:* "Wine is the naturally fermented juice of fresh, ripe grapes. The term "wine" is sometimes used in connection with other products of the soil to denote a beverage made through fermentation, as in *fruit wine, citrus wine, apple wine* and *raisin wine;*" but standing alone it can only mean what Andre L. Simon has called "the living blood of the grape."

Wine made from fruit, by natural fermentation, is deliciously refreshing when well made; and when exceptionally well made, like the extraordinary *Aprivette* made by San Martin Vineyards in the Santa Clara Valley, it carries the fresh bouquet of the fruit along with sipping. But more of this anon.

Our mission, in this chapter, is merely to roam the perimeters of the wine field, sensitively aware to the funky delights to be found in such taste exploration. This is not to deny the rich pleasure of a bottle of California Cabernet Sauvignon with a rare New York cut steak, or a bottle of 1947 Chateau Latour for its glorious depth of character. Let the whole world of wine be your oyster!

And now, about Cold Duck!

I've heard all kinds of stories about the origin of this popular sparkling wine, most of them completely apocryphal. The *real* Cold Duck, known as *Kalte Ente* in Germany, has years of tradition behind it along the Rhine and Mosel rivers, where it is still a festive brew. That's right, it is mixed, contrived, if you will, concocted, like a bowl of punch, in a time-honored method. A spiral peel of lemon is held between the tines of two silver forks in the mouth of a glass pitcher, while a bottle of good Rhine or Mosel-wein is poured over it, and then, for the important sparkle, a bottle of *sekt* (as German champagne is called) like Henkell Trocken splashes over the lemon for the last kiss of the citrus essence. Take away the peel and pour the bubbly concoction from the pitcher . . . it's *Kalte Ente,* or Cold Duck!

Among the legends circulating about the bottled *red* version now so commercially popular, is one about an 18th century German baron in his hunting lodge (shades of Mayerling) who found his cellar short of enough *sekt* to serve all his guests, so he mixed it with some sparkling burgundy—and it was, of course, delicious, and the start of something new. Alas, somewhere along the line that sparkling burgundy became more than slightly sweet. For the general, that did it! If a sweet mixture of champagne and sparkling burgundy is for you, you will enjoy most of the versions of Cold Duck on the market. If you want one slightly less sweet, bottle-fermented, Paul Masson's Very Cold Duck is it.

From another part of the European vineyard comes another popular wine drink of bourgeois origin, called by Burgundians *rince cochon* —"pig rinse." The rather inelegant name for this thirst-quencher was lifted in status by Canon Felix Kir, a popular French resistance leader during World War II. A priest with the distinction of wearing two hats, that of a Bishop of the Church as well as the Mayor of Dijon, improved the quality of the drink, originally a simple white wine, with a spoonful of cassis, by making it with a better base-wine. "Kir" made the pages of *Time* magazine as an "in" drink, when the dry wine involved was Nuits-Saint-Georges "Clos de L'Arlot." Four parts of that fragrant white Burgundy (or another of your choice) to one of Dijon's indigenous crème de cassis makes a truly delightful drink with wine.

From Portugal, a definitely superior pink wine, in a handsome squat bottle, is making all kinds of import records. The label reads MATEUS. Properly it's pronounced *Matt-tay-us,* with the accent on the second syllable, but most people call it *Matt-oose.* Call it anyway you like it, it still tastes good—not great, but good!

There's no law telling you what kind of wine to put in a *weinheber,* that wine dispenser invention of the Austrians. Fill it with Spanada, if you want to, or even better a real red wine from Spain, the Marques De Riscal Rioja. This vintage red from old Castile, in its wire-

43

wrapped Bordeaux-shaped bottle tastes like a good French Claret because 19th century French refugees from phylloxera-stricken vineyards in Bordeaux and Burgundy made their way over the Pyrenees to survive with winemaking. Try it!

Better wine shops may also have bottles of the golden wine of the Magyars, Tokaji-Aszu. Either 3 Puttonos or 5 Puttonos is worth buying wherever you find it, the latter being sweeter, for service with crenshaw melon when summertime arrives. Egri Bikaver, otherwise known as Bull's Blood, is another Hungarian wine worth encountering.

For Maytime, what could be more natural than May Wine? In Germany, this is young, new wine infused with the aromatic leaves and blossoms of the forest shrub, Waldmeister, known to our middle-west as Woodruff. You can buy it already aromatized. Just chill it, use it as a punch-bowl base, floating sliced strawberries around a block of ice.

So, in freedom, back to your Boone's Farm Apple Wine. But don't forget there are really better things in store for you, if you stay on the wine trail, like Romanee-Conti, or, if you insist on white wine with bubbles in it, Taittinger Comtes de Champagne Blanc de Blanc Brut Champagne 1961. If you don't dig it now, you may later.

BOURBON

Five O'Clock High

ON A TRIP TO EUROPE, Mark Twain assured a customs inspector that his luggage contained nothing but clothing. The inspector opened one suitcase and found a bottle of Bourbon inside.

"I thought you said there was only clothing in here," the customs man said.

"I did say that," Mark replied. "You're looking at my nightcap!"

Bourbon is the whiskey of American folklore. Our history is well-laced with the indigenous spirit brewed from corn which the Indians taught the colonists how to grow, distilled with shrewd thrift by the earliest settlers. In the Virginia wilderness that was later to become the state of Kentucky, a Bluegrass preacher named Reverend Elijah Craig blended corn and grain to make whiskey in Bourbon County. It was 1789. The settlers named the region after the great ruling house of France because that country had given so much aid and comfort in the war with England. Reverend Craig was no Timothy Leary of his day; everyone used whiskey in young America. There were no religious sanctions against it. Against abuses, yes; uses, no. Almost every farmer was a distiller. His whiskey was a sovereign remedy for chills or fever, tooth-ache or broken heart. Its sudden fire could also be the quick shot of courage to soften the rough edges of frequently grim, harsh colonial life. When Alexander Hamilton attempted to levy a tax on whiskey to help retire the Revolutionary War debt, the reaction was violent. The arbitrary taxation of George III that led to the Boston Tea Party, that led to the war that gained the Republic, had general remembrance. "The Whiskey Rebellion" gave George Washington some anxious moments, and a few law-abiding, tax-paying farmers were roughed up by more independent neighbors. A few stills were destroyed, a few farmers seized, but the rebellion had no total victory on either side. It did, however, decide two things. The Federal Government established its right to collect taxes for "the common good," and the art of distilling moved into the hills of Kentucky where revenuers weren't so apt to follow. By 1802, the excise tax on domestic spirits was repealed. Kentucky counted more than 2000 distilleries by 1811. A legal industry was well on its way, with a market for grain farmers and large purchases of lumber for fuel, and cooperage.

In 1814, the excise tax on domestic liquor was revived to help finance the War of 1812. The Internal Revenue Bureau was established in 1862 to collect taxes on liquor and other commodities to help defray costs of the Civil War. It was 20¢ a 100-proof gallon then. It's $10.50 per 100-proof gallon today! While the obvious moral is painful, there's a modicum of comfort in knowing the whiskey is better. The Reverend Craig never had it so good, but that formula, to his everlasting credit, still holds for making fine Bourbon: good corn, select grain, pure water, and artful distilling. Wherever a limestone outcropping bubbled with a clearwater spring, barrels of whiskey were sure to grow. The Allegheny Mountains were a barrier to the east, but the whiskey travelled down the Ohio and Mississippi to St. Louis, New Orleans and the South, by keelboats, rafts, and later steamboats. Traders and trappers lugged it along Indian trails. Kegs of Bourbon gurgled in prairie schooners, Conestoga wagons, and Concord coaches heading West. Back in New England, that great orator of the Massachusetts Senate, Daniel Webster, called it his "Kentucky muse." The most time-worn joke of the Civil War was Abraham Lincoln's reply to prohibitionist reformers who complained to him about General Grant's drinking. "I wish I knew what brand of whiskey he drinks so I could give some of it to my other generals," Lincoln said. The story is apparently not apocryphal because a Washington newspaper of July 7, 1863, reported: "President Lincoln today sent his congratulations to General U. S. Grant for his victory at Vicksburg. Included was a gift of a case of fine Bourbon."

FDR mixed his own cocktails every evening in the White House, with a strong preference for a Bourbon Old-Fashioned, but it was not until May 4, 1964, that Congress got around to the adoption of a Resolution singling out Bourbon Whiskey as a "distinctive product of the United States." After almost 200 years, the product of the Kentucky preacher's still became a matter of legal definition: "*Straight Bourbon is a whiskey distilled at not exceeding 160 proof from fermented mash of not less than 51% corn grain, and reduced to 125 proof or less prior to storage in charred, new oak containers for not less than two years—although almost invariably a minimum of four years —and bottled at not less than 80 proof.* No material whatsoever may be added to Bourbon whiskey, *except distilled water to adjust the proof.*"

Chances are, if you're a Bourbon drinker, it'll come as no surprise to learn that fine Bourbon whiskey today is not necessarily a product of Kentucky. It's legally made in a far greater region extending from Pennsylvania south into Tennessee and Virginia, as far west as Illinois, with some production, believe it or not, in Fresno, Sausalito, and Union City, California! Brands have different taste, different flavor, body, bouquet and color for eight different reasons having little to do with geography. Bourbon tastes like it does because:

1. Proportions of grain used to make the fermenting mash vary with brand formulae. A whiskey with corn predominating is light; more barley and rye results in a heavier body requring longer aging.

2. The quality of the grain, particularly the corn and barley malt, must be meticulously selected to make a clean-tasting whiskey.

3. The type and amount of water is as obvious in the making of whiskey as it is in preparing a drink. No decent drink can be made with chemicalized tap water. It's no fetish to make ice-cubes with bottled water. It's the same common sense distillers have recognized since the time of Parson Craig, which produced the phrase "Bourbon and Branch," meaning whiskey and water from a clear spring. Remember, if you're old enough, the crystal clear ice chips you used to snag off the tail-gate of the iceman's wagon? Connoisseurship must include pure water and clear ice today for decent drinks.

4. The character and quality of the yeast makes subtle differences between brands. "*Sour Mash*" is a stupid shibboleth of whiskey snobs. It has little or nothing to do with the taste of the whiskey. It merely means a little of the mash from one lot is used to start the next one. Rightfully, a brand may be certain of continuity of its yeast-culture in this time-honored process of distillation, and so proudly declare its whiskey is made from "Sour Mash," but a "Sweet Mash" whiskey, started up fresh, might taste just the same.

5. "Proof" of the spirit is just now undergoing a revolution by popular truth of taste. Right after the war, when "bootleg" scars were part

of the public experience, "Bottled-in-Bond" had a ring of Government approval—erroneously. It had to be 100 proof, which had nothing, but *nothing* to do with quality. The best drinking whiskey today, American, Scotch, Canadian or Irish, is 86 proof, and taking a page out of the British book, tomorrow's trendsetter will probably be 70 proof! In the words of Jack Baxter, head bartender at that most in-place, Pasadena's Annandale Golf Club, there's almost no demand anymore for 100 proof drinks without walking on your knees.

6. The type of container used for aging, such as charred oak, for mysterious reasons, has much to do with cleansing whiskey flavor. "New white oak" specified in the legal definition of Bourbon, will shortly be amended; white oak is becoming too scarce and expensive, but the change is not major. Whiskey impregnated casks have a premium value in themselves.

7. Would you believe the type of building used for aging storage affects the taste of the whiskey? Kentuckians swear that you can taste the difference between a Bourbon aged in a wooden warehouse with a tin roof, and one stored in a brick building. Temperature control is involved, but in these days of air-conditioning, such horse-and-buggy facilities will soon belong to the antique past.

Bourbon whiskey sales in America account for 51% of the whiskey market, almost double the combined total sales of all foreign whiskey (which, incidentally, are spelled *whisky*, except the Irish, which also uses the "e"), suggesting that, beyond Bourbon, there are other American whiskies adding to the millions of gallons consumed annually. There are 34 types of whiskey, of which straight Bourbon is only one. Jack Daniels is a "Tennessee Sour Mash Whiskey" which, like most other "Tennessee Whiskey," is predominantly, or at least 51%, fermented corn mash. "Blended Whiskey" accounts for most of that other half of whiskey consumption in America. The blender is an artful master, using select straight whiskies, with neutral grain spirits to produce a light, harmonious, uniform-tasting product to brand specifications. Regulations permit up to 2½% by volume of blending materials. The most common is a heavy, sweet Spanish Sherry made from the Pedro Ximenez grape.

Bartender Baxter explained to us that Easterners in common parlance refer to all blended whiskey as "Rye," but this is purely regional colloquialism. Given a shot of real "Rye Whiskey" they'd get a heavy shock! Taste today is more honestly for lighter, more palate-pleasing beverages that don't give the Five O'Clock palate a medicinal blast. How often have you watched regulars at a bar take aboard their first drink of the day with an expression that clearly says only *"Ungawa!"*? Those days are happily drawing to an end.

Originally, *"highball"* described a ball raised as a signal for railroad trains to go ahead, or speed up. When saloon barkeeps realized that ice, Bourbon, and water could be mixed with speed, they called it a "highball." That didn't say anything about how good it tasted. In the 1870's, when the American-born Lady Churchill, Sir Winston's mother, was the reigning belle of New York society, she staged a dinner in honor of Samuel J. Tilden's election as Governor, and introduced a new cocktail—a mixture of Bourbon, sweet Vermouth, and a dash of bitters. It was named after the exclusive club where it was served—The Manhattan.

Mint Juleps, in frosty silver tumblers notwithstanding, Bourbon is at its most delicious best in the sweet and elegant Manhattan. The "Perfect Manhattan" is well named, moderating the sweetness, *stirring* half sweet and half dry vermouth, with an equal measure of Bourbon, and a dash of bitters. The one-to-one formula, Bourbon and vermouth, is classic, but many true whiskey palates prefer as much as four- or five-to-one. The stemmed cherry garnish is classic, and a twist of orange peel optional. After all, no one drinks words or recipes. How does the result taste—to *you*?

How long has it been, Mr. Scotch Drinker, since you've had a Perfect Manhattan? Chances are, a well-made Manhattan can eliminate that Five O'Clock shudder with the first drink!

Try some of these for *auld lang syne:*

OLD FASHIONED: ½ lump sugar, 2 dashes of bitters and then add enough water to cover sugar. Muddle well in old fashioned glass. Next comes 1 cube ice and 2 ounces Bourbon. Stir well, add twist of lemon rind and drop in glass. For color, decorate with slices of orange, lemon and cherry. Serve with stir rod.

MANHATTAN: 1 dash bitters, ¾ ounce Sweet Vermouth, and 1½ ounces Bourbon. Stir well with cracked ice, strain slowly into 3 ounce cocktail glass, and serve with a bright red cherry.

BOURBON SOUR: Juice of ½ fresh lemon, ½ teaspoon powdered sugar, and 2 ounces Bourbon. Shake well with cracked ice and strain into 6 ounce Bourbon Sour glass. Decorate with a half-slice of lemon and one cherry.

BOURBON MIST: Fill an old fashioned glass with finely crushed ice, add 2 jiggers of Bourbon and top with a twist of lemon peel.

MINT JULEP: Muddle 2 sprigs of mint, 1 lump sugar and one table-spoon water in a tall glass or tankard. Fill with crushed ice and add 2 ounces Bourbon. Do not stir. Garnish with fresh mint sprig. Perfect harmony for summer time.

THE ALL-AMERICAN: 4 parts cranberry juice, 2 parts Bourbon, 1 part light Virgin Islands rum, and 1 part lime or lemon juice. Serve in an old-fashioned glass with 2 cubes of ice. Important! Stir, do not shake.

BOURBON FOG: For the Christmas season or after a football game, combine 1 quart strong, chilled coffee, 1 quart Bourbon, and 1 quart vanilla ice cream. Put in punch bowl and stir away. Truly enchanting. Truly delicious.

SAZERAC COCKTAIL: 2 heavy-bottomed 3½-ounce bar glasses are required. Fill one with cracked ice and let chill. In the other, moisten a lump of sugar and crush with a spoon. Add several drops of Peychaud's bitters, a quick dash of Angostura and a generous shot of Bourbon. Add several ice cubes and stir, don't shake. Empty the first glass of its ice, dash in several drops of herbsaint, twirl the glass and shake out the flavorful herbsaint. Strain into this glass the whiskey mixture, twist in a drop of oil from a lemon peel and serve. Do not drop the peel into the drink. They're still talking about this one in the bars of the French Quarter.

THE COLORADO HAILSTORM: This authentic drink of the Early West is served in pint mason jars. The cap is screwed on securely and

The Taste of Our American Heritage . . .

THE STORY IS TOLD of the young Frank Lloyd Wright, as a child in Wisconsin. The family farm was far out in the country. Isolation and heavy winter snows often invoked disciplines which the noted achitectural designer's father imposed sternly.

On the morning of the incident recalled, a new-fallen snow whitened the reach of land stretching between the farmhouse and the woodshed. Taking the mittened hand of the young toddler, the elder Wright made a straight line through the fresh snow to the woodshed. Midway, the little boy slipped his hand out of the mitten in his father's grasp, and struck out on a wide circular path to clumps of frosted weeds, sparkling in the sun like crystal flowers. Gathering them from here and there into a bouquet, he arrived at the woodshed where his father was waiting.

Pointing to the straight line of his steps leading from the house, intersected by the random zigzag pattern of the boy's steps, he spoke: "Straight is the way!" The little boy looked up at his father, and wistfully down to the bouquet of snow-transformed beauty in his hand.

That's all there is to the story. The grown child's accomplishments in the world still stand in many quarters, not only as inspiration to rising generations of young architects, but as striking evidence that the unimaginative, direct, straight path is *not* the only way. The course of the individualist may be an even richer experience.

Non sequitur to the subject of rye whiskey? I think not, especially today. Like those rugged souls who smoke Camels, there's a strong determination to seek out the full, grainy flavor of rye by those discriminating customers at the bar, calling for whiskey drinks, prefaced with "rye." A "Rye-Manhattan" or a "Rye-Old Fashioned," several decades ago, would have been redundant expressions. The originals were conceived with old-line American whiskies, which were predominantly blends of grain whiskey, largely rye.

Popular tastes and drink nomenclature are regional, and not without a debt to history.

In an attempt to reduce the Revolutionary war debt, Alexander Hamilton arbitrarily settled upon a whiskey tax as a primary source of revenue. Practically every one used whiskey, and most farmers made it. The reaction was violent! Still smarting from the imposed taxes of George III which had set off the grand conflict that brought about the independence of the colonies, the fledgling nation's war debt was of even less concern to the general public than it is today. By 1794, Hamilton had to appeal to President Washington to send out the militia. When they marched into Pennsylvania, the "Whiskey Rebellion" was on!

Farmer-distillers, in some areas, headed for the hills, to avoid the revenue agents. Some followed the pioneer trails over the Appalachians into Kentucky. There, they got a taste of the corn-whiskey created by the Reverend Elijah Craig. By 1810 there were 2,000 stills at work in Bourbon County, producing Kentucky's new Bourbon Whiskey.

Those farmers who remained behind the emigration south, continued in their tradition of distilling malted grains from a fermented mash of largely rye. That was *real* whiskey! The basic taste was there, soft, full, glorious, and rich! Some other farmers trekked west by the waterway to Ohio, and wherever they could find sweet springs of fresh water. On the face of the famed Old Overholt label today, you can read the founding date of that Ohio distillery, 1810. They weren't making the new "Bourbon" whiskey, they were making *whiskey;* but is was from rye, not corn predominantly. The taste for whiskey in Pennsylvania and New York continued to be rye. Inevitably, the lighter, golden corn whiskey of the Reverend Craig's great mash from Bourbon County, from areas of limestone brooks, made the "branch water" whiskey the reigning favorite of the West, with in-roads upon the East. Today, 78 million gallons of Bourbon are consumed annually, but there are still customers calling for 1 million gallons of rye every year.

Canadian whiskey has rye in the malted grains, but there is also corn, wheat, and barley. Proportions of each grain are the trade secrets of each distillery.

The predominant grain in the fermented mash make-up determines the label-designation of the whiskey. If it is 51% or more rye, it makes a "straight rye"; 51% or more of corn produces "bourbon." Both are distilled at 160 proof, and then reduced by the addition of the all-important pure water, at the time of bottling, to not less than 80 proof.

"Blended rye whiskey" is blended whiskey which contains not less than 51% by volume of straight rye whiskey. The rest, in most of the blends is, frankly, Bourbon, as the Bourbon Institute is happy to point out.

The man who pours Wild Turkey Rye at his bar you just know to be positive of his taste, an interesting maverick, and he'll pour a good drink! The fellow who adds a dash of Amer Picon to his Old Fashioned, and gives it a touch of cherry brandy, emphasizing the zing with a few drops of kirsch skimming the surface, has some status going for him. He's in the same league with the martini-buff who rinses out his cocktail glass, before pouring, with absinthe. Here and there you may find Old Mr. Boston Rock & Rye, good whiskey with a string of rock-candy, pure sugar crystals visibly there inside the bottle. It has fans that will tell you it's a cold remedy *par excellence!* So's a hot toddy! But don't make it in a straight-line recipe—add those extra, off-beat "flowers," maybe brown sugar instead of white, lemon juice *plus* a touch of orange, muddle with a stick of cinnamon, titillate with more complex spicing, like a few specks of allspice and a final dusting with fresh grated nutmeg. Since colonial days, when the toddy was given its final polish with the thrust of a hot poker, a lump of butter just before serving was not amiss.

The Bourbon Institute unveiled its list of the 10 top drinks in America recently. Bartenders have contests every year for new drinks, but the 10 which have stood the test of time are:

Bourbon and water	Highball
Mint Julep	Sazerac
Manhattan	Egg Nog
Old Fashioned	Stone Fence
Bourbon Sour	Hot Toddy

Only two in the list may seem esoteric, the Stone Fence and the Sazerac, but they're both old-timers. Washington Irving claimed, in 1809, that the Stone Fence was a drink conceived by the Dutch settlers. Not bad, either. It's just whiskey, cider, and ice. A tall tumbler filled loosely with ice, plus a jigger of Bourbon or Rye, then filled with apple cider. Now there's cider, and cider! A good, fresh, cold, country apple cider laced with smooth rye has gotta be something else! In case you've forgotten, a Sazerac is Bourbon, or Rye, if you wish, with a teaspoon of sugar muddled in an Old-Fashioned glass with a couple dashes of aromatic bitters, to which 2 dashes of absinthe precede 1½ jiggers of whiskey, twists of lemon and orange peel, and stirring around ice cubes.

There you have it! The legend of rye whiskey in America. Diminishing in popularity, giving place to lighter whiskey, but appreciated fully by individualists seeking something better just off the beaten track. With rye, its ardent fans would claim, you can make the *Most* Perfect Manhattan.

Additional Recipes

The Golden Aqua of Scotland
SCOTCH

MAN WAS A LONG TIME in perfecting the sorcery of the alembic, in producing a gold elixir of life from the lowly grains of the field. The origins of the art of distillation have Egyptian tracery weaving the antique name of that mysterious land into the equally dark word—*alchemy*. This was an occult art, but in cloistered studies, there was sincere searching for an *elixir vitae*, a universal medicine which might cure all disease and indefinitely prolong life. Thomas Aquinas was among the alchemists of the 13th century, and, to his Italian contemporary, Arnoldus de Villa Nova, is given the earliest credit for producing *aqua vitae* from wine, which we call *brandy*. Far to the north, in the Caledonian highlands, Malcolm, the Vicar of Keith, was producing a "heather ale" as a monkish prerogative, and while that secret formula is lost from those 13th century times, those Gaelic scholars, echoing their churchly Latin backgrounds, brought us our common word "Whisky," from their Celtic *uisge beatha*, for *aqua vitae*, or "water of life." As the centuries rolled by, the distilled spirit of the heather-clad moors became known to the English who shaped the Celtic word to their own tongue's comfort, and *uisge* became "whiskey." The Scots spelled it that way—*whisky*, but the Irish, who also had learned the arts of distillation, insisted upon inserting an "e"—"whiskey," but our neighbors to the north, in Canada, call their elixir of cereal grain, "whisky."

As early as 1545, the privilege of distilling had left the church in Scotland. One George Ogilvy of Miltoun obtained a grant of lands from the Bishop of Moray, including the "Brasina," the brewhouse of Keith. It stood on the present site of the Strathisla-Glenlivet Distillery which today produces one of the Highland malt "singles" which is important to the prestigious Chivas Regal.

But that's getting ahead of our story. We intend to tell you how Scotch Whisky is made, what it IS, and even why it tastes like it does, but the concentration of history around the whisky business in the last

150 years is most revealing and significant, for this innocent *aqua vitae* was to become one of the sinews of war and taxation, the foundation of great fortunes and from a common, inexpensive, pungent, smoky beverage, to emerge as a golden nectar, of liqueur mellowness, a sometimes status drink, with brands of fashion.

On the 14th of August in 1822, King George IV of England stepped ashore in Leith, Scotland, on a voyage of goodwill and conciliation, the first royal appearance since Bonnie Prince Charlie's ill-fated attempt in 1745 to win back the throne of his fathers. Greeted by Sir Walter Scott, his Majesty called for a bottle of Highland whisky to drink the poet's health in the national liquor. It had only been a few years earlier, in 1814, that all whiskies became subject to tax, and distillation in stills of less than 500 gallon capacity had been prohibited. As almost every Scottish chieftan presided over his own *aqua vitae* still, and drank it with proprietary gusto, the law had almost caused a revolution. But the more important trade, which George IV's visit accented, was the shipping tie with France and the continent, for the wine merchants on the docks of Leith. Long in feudal fealty to Edinburgh, Leithers rejoiced in being recognized as the royal port of Scotland. Among those early shipping houses were two that would emerge in the whisky trade, and endure, Andrew Usher and William Sanderson. Gladstone, as Prime Minister, survived the fear of a French invasion, in 1859, and mended international fences with a French free trade treaty which would alter the course of the wine and spirits trade. "The alliance with France is the true basis of peace in Europe," he declared, "for England and France will never unite in any European purpose which is radically unjust." Britain reduced duties on wines and brandies, and paid for this extravagance of free-trade theories by raising the excise tax on British-made spirits to 10 shillings per proof gallon. That was the beginning. With each war that was to come in the ensuing decades, the tax on spirits would climb. By 1947, it was called again, to rescue the British pound, having reached a total of one hundred and ninety shillings and tenpence per proof gallon! Happily for the coffers of Britannia, production, export and consumption figures in one century had zoomed even more astronomically.

When William Sanderson determined to enter the wine and spirits trade on Charlotte Lane in Leith, in 1863, spirit sales were in a kind of doldrums. Wines and cordials were more popular. Highland whiskies, Lowland whiskies, and the pungent, smoky Islay spirits had little more than local fame. Sanderson paid five guineas for the privilege of being a "dealer" in "made wines": Rich Green Ginger Wine, Ginger Cordial, Rhubarb Wine, Raspberry Cordial, and even a liqueur called "Parfait Amour." Studying his trade as a rectifier, compounding flavoring materials and essences, he came upon a text: *"The prevalent notion amongst Whisky drinkers, especially in Scotland, is that several varieties of Whisky blended is superior to that of any one kind."* Thinking to add "Mixture Whisky" to his line of cordials and liqueurs, his record book has the first "recipe" for a blended Scotch whisky:

> "10 gallons Glenlivet, 10 gallons Pitlochry
> 5 gallons Reduced mixed Aqua, 8 gallons Grain
> 4 gallons water, ½ gallon Aqua Shrub
> 8 gallons Grain Aqua."

The "Aqua" is, of course, not water, but Scotch whisky. His notebooks also revealed that *"Whisky stored in Sherry casks soon acquires a mellow softness which it does not get when put into new casks; in fact, the latter, if not well-seasoned, will impart a woodiness, much condemned by the practised palate. In Sherry casks, the spirit likewise acquires a pleasing tinge of colour which is much sought for."*

Mr. Sanderson's "Mixture Whisky" became exceedingly popular, and his trade flourished. The Victorian era was coming into full flower. His friend, John Begg, founded Lochnagar distillery neighboring the Queen's favorite haunt, Balmoral.

The development of high-yield patent stills greatly increased gallonage for an expanding market, but the art of blending with pot still whisky still remained with individual wine and spirits merchants, like Sanderson. Sales were made in casks, both to households and to public houses, for reduction, with water, by the owner. Some bottled it themselves. Sanderson's son pointed out the possible disadvantages to the reputation of their house by the carelessness or ignorance of either consumer or other retailer, and came up with an answer that has made more than one fortune: "Bottle it!" But which one? With almost one hundred blends in separate casks and vats, he decided to leave this decision to a panel of skilled blenders. Their choice was unanimous for the vat numbered 69. VAT 69 is probably one of the earliest brands of Scotch whisky in commercial trade.

In these early days, Sanderson and other blenders and merchants bought their findings in an open market. As their business grew, they had some trepidation that they might not be able to control their sources of supply. The boom in Scotch whisky, with the advent of blending, now reached an expanding export market. The rough edges of the indigenous Highland spirit were softened with Lowland malt and grain whiskies from the patent stills. Moving with intensity, Sanderson, and a fellow Leither, Robert Harvey Thomson, along with Andrew Usher, John Crabbie and John Begg, and several others of the Royal Lochnagar distillery, in December 1885 founded The Distillers Company Limited, a cooperative enterprise, creating the world's largest distillery. Today, in its roster of A-blends, that parent company controls VAT 69, Haig & Haig, Johnnie Walker, Dewar's White Iabel, Black & White, White Horse, and King George IV, the latter being the instant nucleus for the whole combine. The famous brands grew, not from individual distilleries, but from wine and spirits traders and merchants, houses catering to both crown and publican, the earliest being of Scottish origin. Berry Brothers, in London, "At the Sign of the Coffee Mill" in St. James' Street, across from the Palace, weighed in, in its "chair scale," the notorious friend of the Prince Regent, Beau Brummel. It would later provide, in addition to the most choice wines of the continent, a Scotch whisky named after a swift sailing clipper ship, the *Cutty Sark!*

The seeming boom was not without crises, and with the post World War I increasing extravagant rates of duty, an economic crisis deepened year by year. In 1930 production dropped from 21 million proof gallons to 16 million proof gallons, and in 1932 to only 9 million proof gallons. Distilleries were either only partly working or closed down. Only fifteen distilleries out of the 156 that began the century were left working! You guessed it. America repealed Prohibition, and the tide turned! Today, more than 2 million cases of Cutty Sark alone are exported to the USA, and as many for J&B, the status-brand from London's wine merchants, Justerini & Brooks. Chivas Regal, with a high price, moves more than 500,000 cases annually to the prestige market in America. It's no secret that the Kennedy fortune rode high on the crest of the post-repeal whisky wave, when father Joseph got the inside track with his good connections at home and abroad as FDR became President, appointing the financier as Ambassador to Great

Britain in those significant 30's. In 1937, the prodigious Seagrams Company began to build vast libraries of rare Scotch whiskies, acquiring both lands and buildings in Scotland. In 32 years, the Distillers Corporation-Seagrams Limited reached $1 billion in sales and assets, their handsome distilleries in Scotland thriving with Chivas Regal, 100 Pipers, Passport, Sherrif's Premium, and Royal Salute being well established, inviting attention to a new liqueur for the Scotch taste—Lochan Ora, subtly produced by "Chivas Brothers Ltd." So, what began as barely respectable alchemistry in the Dark Ages' search for an *elixir vitae,* emerged from the cloisters to the laboratories of dabbling wine and spirits merchants, raising whisky blending to an art of such magnificent acceptance it could establish family dynasties, supply an export market exceeding 30 million gallons per year, and support the very currency of the government which taxed it into its precious price.

A look into that mutual action of barley and water, smoke and fire, which uses nature as the activating agent, will tell us a little more about this golden *aqua vitae* of Scotland, separating fact from fancy. It might even cause a little brand switching to learn some of the basics involved, and to prize an inexpensive Scotch like King George IV for its true merit and history, as possibly one of the best bargains among the DCL brands!

"What IS Whisky?" became the subject of legal enquiry, in 1905, at Islington, London, when, under the Disraeli 1875 Sale of Food and Drugs Act, a magistrate ruled that the blending of pot still Whisky and patent still spirit, as grain whisky was then called, was not Whisky. It took a royal commission, and an excited general public to press the case to final findings, which emerged in July 1909: "Our general conclusion, therefore, on the part of our inquiry is that 'Whisky' is a spirit obtained by distillation from a mash of cereal grains saccharified by the diastase of malt; that 'Scotch Whisky' is Whisky, as above defined, distilled in Scotland; and that Irish Whiskey is Whiskey, as above defined, distilled in Ireland."

And now, here's how the native spirit of Scotland is made. There are five basic steps in the production of fine quality malt whiskies:

1. MALTING, in which the barley is dressed, sieved, and screened to eliminate any inferior grains. Then it is soaked in water tanks, called "steeps." Spread out in the "Saladin boxes" of the malting house, each

65

separate grain begins to sprout, to germinate in the low-ceilinged, warm rooms and lofts. When the sprouts are slightly less than an inch long, the humidifying experience is over; the grain is now known as "green malt." Malt is germinated grain. The miraculous transformation has already occurred in the chemical constituency of the grain which will make fermentation possible. The natural starches have been changed into diastase, which can convert the remaining starch into sugars, maltose and dextrin, which, by the agent of yeast, produces alcohol. Starch in its original form cannot.

The green malt is laid over a screen floor directly over smoking peat fire. In this kiln it takes on that earthy incense from the peat smoke which will be transmitted to the ultimate whisky, identifying it as a true Scottish malt whisky.

2. MASHING simply is making a mush from dried, ground green malt by mixing it with warm water until all the diastase has turned the starches into sugar which are dissolved in the water, now called *wort*.

3. FERMENTING is accomplished by the addition of cultivated pure yeast. Just as yeasts act upon the juice of grapes to make wine, they act upon the *wort*, producing alcohol, and carbonic acid gas, producing a liquid known as "beer" or *wash*. If there had been hops in the *wort*, it might indeed have been real beer or ale.

4. DISTILLING takes place in an onion-shaped copper pot still, which is fired up to vaporize the *wash*. The first distillate comes from the condenser of low alcoholic strength, and is called the *low wine*. The first and last parts of this first distillation, known as the *heads* and *tails* or *feints*, are kept separate from the valuable middle portion. The beginning and end of the distillation is apt to have impurities, lodged in the *feints*, which would lower the quality of flavor of the *aqua* ultimately. The *feints*, however, are returned to the spirits still to recover their useful alcohol.

The fine spirits, distilled at 140 to 142 proof are now whisky, and flow into spirit safes for visual checking, and then into a spirit vat, from which they are put into oak barrels, usually Sherry casks.

5. MATURING whisky in barrels has been reduced with spring water to 124 to 126 proof. Every distiller becomes a poet when he

talks about the water that is in his whisky. One stream will differ from another because of winds that sigh across the heather and caress the rock-tumbled rapids. And science bears them out. Two of the Seagram distilleries in Scotland made a research experiment, briefly using each other's water supply, all else remaining equal. The whiskies were excellent but different! So, the banksides of peat, or the woody glens and heathery moors are more than mere poetry for the golden *aqua*.

All whisky warehouses in Scotland have two locks. One can be opened only by Government Excise Officers, and the other by the distillery's warehouse staff. The whiskies are in bond, with duty still to be paid, when the spirits are taken out. This is happily the case, because the Scotch industry loses about 11 million gallons of whisky per year merely by evaporation!

All whisky sold in the British Isles must be over three years of age, and that imported into the USA from either Scotland or Ireland must be at least four years old if it does not contain an age statement on the label.

Samuel Bronfman, the late acknowledged dean of the world-wide distilling industry, when President of the Seagram empire, tersely described the most important step in the production of fine Scotch whisky: "Distilling is a science; blending is an art." An artist may work with three basic colors, red, yellow, and blue to create the entire rainbow palette, or its greyed variations. The musician has the limited range of an octave, but 35 different musical instruments to compose his statement. Scotch whisky blenders can assemble examples from 123 distilleries, from 5 different types: *Highland Malt*, the most expensive, with a gentle smokiness; *Lowland Malt*, light in body, mild in flavor; *Campbelltown Malt*, very full bodied and heavy with smoke; *Islay Malt*, off the southwest coast, very full bodied, pungent, peaty and aggressively flavored; and *Grain Whisky*, produced differently, in continuous stills, from a mixture of maize (corn) and malted and unmalted barley—of higher proof, lighter and less insistent.

All of these are the "singles" which, when selected and blended, go to make up the more than 4000 brands and blends the market affords. The secret of the best Scotch lies in the art of the blender. One fine liqueur blend, which merely means it is truly aged and mellow, may contain as many as 30 or 40 different malt whiskies, and several grain whiskies of varying age. All will be matured beyond three or four years before the blending marriage, and have yet another aging before being bottled. A whisky which announces a 12-year age on its label is not necessarily better than one with no age statement, nor is one that is pale in color lighter in body than the more golden Scotch. Today, for uniformity, caramel is added merely for color control, but how many "connoisseurs" have told you how they prefer a "light Scotch" and point to the color for their evidence? Even truly fine, old Scotch may not be the choice of true connoisseurs.

Several years ago, after taking a tour of Kilmarnock House, the headquarters of Johnnie Walker Scotch Whiskies in Scotland, we arrived with the Export Director in the elegant, oak-panelled Board Room, and were invited to have a taste of the product. "What will you have?" might have seemed a simple question, when there were only two possible answers, Red Label or Black Label, but I turned the invitation back to my host. "Which do YOU drink?" I asked. A measured pause preceded his reply. "In America," he replied, "the Black Label is considered the best because it is the more expensive. We drink the Red Label. It has more zwang on the palate."

Zwang on the palate! Maybe that's what a true Scotch drinker keeps looking for. In stores that sell the heavily kilned *Laphroaig,* one of the very few unblended Scotches, customers ask for it with a certain bravura; they know the smoky taste of Islay Malt Whisky, and like it. Cafe Society and theatrical personalities who followed the pace of Charlie Burns at New York's "21" made Ballantine's, then unknown in Europe, an in-drink, and now a leading label in all the jet-set bars of the world.

The phenomenal rise in popularity of the Vodka Martini over the gin original, since World War II, points to an American taste for lighter, neutral to non-existent flavor. Scotch blends also reflect the same trend to lightness and bland taste. The light-bodied Scotches are less expensive to produce, with more grain whisky and less of the costly Highland malt whiskies. That's where the status drinker is headed if Scotch is his thing. But if you're a real Scotch drinker, and love the poetry of peat incense, maybe it's time to taste old VAT 69 again, or King George IV, or look for Laphroaig. They're the primary golden *aqua* of Scotland!

You might rightly shudder at the thought of Scotch-and-7-Up, but these recipes have traditions in taste offensive only to rock-ribbed purists:

SCOTCH HIGHBALL: This tall, iced drink consists of a generous jigger (or more) of Scotch whiskey over 2-3 ice cubes and enough carbonated water to nearly fill the highball glass. Use a glass stirring rod to stir quickly and lightly. Bourbon can be substituted, as well as cold water instead of the carbonated water.

ROB ROY: Combine ½ ounce sweet vermouth and 3 ounces Scotch in a mixing glass and fill with 6-8 ice cubes. Stir gently to chill and dilute the drink. Then place a strainer on top of the mixing glass and pour into a 4-ounce cocktail glass. Twist an orange peel strip over the glass to release the oil, twirl the cut edge of the peel around the inside rim of the glass, and add the peel to the drink. Use a light Scotch preferably. To make a dry Rob Roy, change the proportions to 3½ ounces of Scotch and 1 teaspoon of dry vermouth.

SCOTCH SOUR: Refer to the Bourbon recipe. Just substitute Scotch.

SAZERAC: Refer to the Bourbon recipe. Just substitute Scotch.

OLD FASHIONED: Refer to the Bourbon recipe. Just substitute Scotch.

SCOTCH MIST: Refer to the Bourbon Mist recipe. Just substitute Scotch.

MANHATTAN: Refer to the Bourbon recipe. Just substitute Scotch.

MINT JULEP: Refer to the Bourbon recipe. Just substitute Scotch.

RUSTY NAIL: For a tasteful after-dinner drink, combine 1½ ounces Scotch with 1½ ounces Drambuie in an old-fashioned glass. Add 2 ice cubes and stir gently. Refreshing, isn't it?

MORNING GLORY: Combine 1½ ounces lemon juice and 1 teaspoon superfine sugar in a mixing glass, and stir with a bar spoon to dissolve the sugar. Add 2½ ounces Scotch, 6 drops Pernod, 1 egg white, 2 teaspoons heavy cream and 3-4 ice cubes. Place a shaker on top of the mixing glass and, grasping them firmly together with both hands, shake vigorously 6 or 7 times. Remove the shaker, place a strainer on top of the mixing glass, and pour into a 6-ounce cocktail glass (well chilled).

CAMERON'S KICK COCKTAIL: Combine ¾ ounce Scotch, ¾ ounce Irish whiskey, juice of ¼ lemon and 2 dashes of orange bitters. Shake well with cracked ice and strain into 3-ounce cocktail glass. Quite a kick!

Additional Recipes

GIN

After Three Centuries...a Matter of Taste

NO MATTER HOW ERUDITE THE TEXT, the story of gin rocks with ribald and vulgar history, because the naked spirit became the national drink of England one short century after its more noble origins in Holland. The juniper-flavored spirit was no accident; it was the brain-child of a 17th century professor of medicine at the University of Leyden, one Franciscus de la Boe (1614-1672), *aka* Doctor Sylvius.

Mother Nature has provided us with no more potent diuretic than the blue-purple berry of the *juniperus communis*, an evergreen as common in Kamchatka, Persia, the Alps and the Pyrenees, as in the Himalayas and the Sierra Nevada! Small wonder that Dr. Sylvius was able to obtain juniper berries, extract their oil, and by redistilling pure alcohol in concert, achieve a new and relatively inexpensive medicine. He called it *Genièvre*, the French word for "juniper." To the Dutch, it became *genever*, which it remains as "Geneva Gin," and the English made a quick cop-out of the word, emerging from soldiers who'd fought on the Continent, as "gin," short for the "Dutch Courage" popularly distilled near Rotterdam.

Booze and politics are often bedfellows, united by tax appeal. The quarrel with the French by the English, under Queen Anne, continued the restrictions on French wines and brandies, encouraging English distillers with lower excise taxes. Everybody could afford English gin! And did! You could get drunk for a penny—and dead-drunk for tu' pence! Painters and engravers were the pictorial journalists of the day. The times were robust and raucous, the streets of London a rather bawdy bedlam reported in "Harlot's Progress," "Gin Lane," and "A Rake's Progress" by William Hogarth (1697-1764) with as much fidelity to detail as today's television cameras, albeit with slightly more satire in his series of scenes which he called "a dumb show." The pock-splotched and debauched, rich and poor caricatured by Hogarth were in this depraved state largely because gin was cheap and available. It got its subtitle, *"Mother's Ruin,"* in the 18th century. The bathtub gin of the Prohibition era of the 1920's in the U.S.A. didn't do much more to make gin a respectable drink, in spite of the fact that the Martini was born a stone's throw from San Francisco in 1860, with eminent respectability.

Without the disaster of Prohibition to scar its evolution in the British Isles, gin made great refining strides in England, to become a beverage of fashion in the Mauve Decade. *Gin and It* would never have become *apéritif* tradition of the English unless the spirit had made bold and brilliant improvements over the "Dutch Courage" brew distilled after the Restoration.

Today there are two basic kinds of gin: *Holland,* or *Dutch Gin,* which is distilled at a low proof (100 to 110 proof) from "malt wine" of barley, corn, and rye in equal parts and redistilled with juniper berries, in pot stills at 94 to 98 proof; and *Dry Gin,* the refined *English* gin, distilled in a column still from 75 per cent corn, 15 per cent barley malt, and 10 per cent of other grains. The resulting pure spirit is 180 to 188 proof. This is reduced with distilled water to 120 proof, then redistilled in a pot still, the vapors rising through a screen holding a secret collection of "botanicals" including juniper berries, plus the distiller's own chosen formula possibly drawn from anise, orris root, licorice, coriander and caraway seeds, cassia bark, cocoa beans, lemon and orange peel. The rising vapors absorb the essential oils of the chosen aromatics and descend through cooling condenser coils flavored as gin at 170 to 180 proof.

The only difference between English and American gin is found in the choice of "botanicals," the taste of the water used in making the mash fermentation, and the final difference in bottled proof, which is slightly lower in the English product.

Gin does not need age to make it smooth or palatable; it's ready to be bottled for use when it comes from the still, upon reduction with distilled water. Usually it is stored in glass-lined tanks, but an occasional producer ages the spirit in wood, from which it takes on a golden color.

There's every reason for brand preferences when it comes to gin! I still agree that "Drinks Never Taste Thin With Gordon's Gin" and it makes a good classical Martini! There's unquestionable prestige where Booth's House of Lords Gin is poured, and equally for Lloyd's Distilled

London Dry, which boasts of its fresh orange and lemon peel accent in its "botanicals." Fleischmann's, Gilbey's, Schenley's, Seagram's and Hiram Walker are standard reliable products, but fashion seems to favor fancier gins like Tanqueray with its uniquely shaped bottle and red seal, Bombay Gin with its own tantalizing nuance of taste, and Boodles British Gin with that name you can't forget! Today's status champion, however, for the all-time favorite, is James Burroughs' famed Beefeater Gin. It's no PR flak—one member of the Burroughs family personally attends the measuring of the ingredients for each batch of botanicals when the Beefeater Gin is distilled in Lambeth. A triple distillation makes this premium product the far cry it is from the crude spirits of Hogarth's *Gin Lane* two centuries back.

And now, about that Martini cocktail!

Authorities seem to agree that San Francisco, or rather near-by Martinez, was honored by Jerry Thomas, the bartender of a bay city hotel who published his original gin and vermouth recipe in *The Bon Vivant's Companion* in 1862. There's little point in re-publishing that recipe. Suffice it to say it had gin and vermouth, plus bitters, maraschino and ice, was stirred and served with a quarter-slice of lemon. But there *is* a major reason for pointing out why there's an intriguing taste-truth to be achieved in relating to the "botanicals" in a superb Martini. Because *any* Martini, no matter whether it's a pre-World War II 4 to 1 mix, or today's 15 to 1 shot with only a shadow of a vermouth bottle, *any* Martini needs a superior gin as its send-off. The fellow who rinses his cocktail glass with Pernod before pouring the Martini into it, is pointing to the absinthe flavors of anise, orris root, and licorice which *could* be among the "botanicals." My friend, the late film star Rod La Rocque, prided himself on his Martini learned in his De Mille days, which attractively stirred a spiral peel of a whole lemon in a 4 to 1 formula featuring a fine French vermouth and a beautiful British gin! The olive in the Martini is a little more than an hors d'oeuvre; it has residual flavor if eaten first, to tilt the taste of subsequent sips. The pearl onion does perhaps the same thing for the Gibson.

As the indigenous environment for the Martini, San Francisco follows the international trend which has taken the Dry Martini cocktail from an artful blending of gin and aromatic vermouth to a euphemistic call-title for a naked hooker of the most neutral hootch-on-the-rocks! The vodka martini is a pale pretender; it's only a polite way of asking for a quick shot of bracing booze. Some connoisseurs in the same league order gin, equally unadorned. These are the folks who really can tell you which bottled brand has the best "botanicals"! It is, after three centuries of refinement, a matter of taste.

Fashions in drinks move more slowly through the calendar than hemlines or shoulder-shapes, but every now and then a drink does gain the status of style—like the *Negroni* imported from the sophisticated circles of Rome.

GIN GIMLET: Refer to Vodka recipes. Just substitute Gin.

GIN SCREWDRIVER: Refer to Vodka recipes. Just substitute Gin.

GIN MARTINI: Refer to Vodka recipes. Just substitute Gin.

GIN BLOODY MARY: Refer to Vodka recipes. Just substitute Gin.

GIN & TONIC: Place 2 ice cubes in a highball glass and add 3 ounces Gin. Fill glass with 4-6 ounces cold Quinine water and garnish with a slice of lemon or lime. Do not stir.

NEGRONI: Into a 6-ounce old-fashioned glass, place 2 ice cubes. Add 1½ ounces Carpano or sweet vermouth, 1½ ounces Campari bitters, 1½ ounces Gin. Stir the ingredients together briefly and drop in 1 strip lemon peel. A very popular international cocktail.

TOM COLLINS: This tall drink combines 1 ounce fresh lemon juice, 3 ounces Gin and 1½ teaspoons superfine sugar. Stir with a bar spoon and dissolve the sugar. Add 2 ice cubes, fill glass with 6 ounces cold club soda and stir briefly. Garnish the drink, if you wish, with an orange slice and/or a cherry. Liquors such as rum, bourbon, vodka or Scotch can be substituted for the Gin.

GIN & BITTERS: To 1 ice cube, just add a dash of Angostura bitters and 3 ounces Gin. Have a 4-ounce glass well chilled in advance. A simple, but effective recipe.

SINGAPORE SLING: Combine 2 ice cubes (whole or cracked), ½ ounce Cherry Heering or cherry brandy, ½ ounce fresh lemon juice and 3 ounces Gin in a highball glass. Fill the glass with cold water and stir. You can substitute club soda for the water and thus it becomes a Singapore Rickey.

ROSE COCKTAIL: Also known as a French Manhattan, one combines 2 dashes of Fiel's orange bitters, ½ ounce sweet vermouth, ½ ounce dry vermouth, ½ ounce cherry brandy and ½ ounce kirsch. Add 1 ounce Gin and put in a 4-ounce cocktail glass and stir very gently so as not to cloud it. Twist 1 strip orange peel over the glass to release the oil and then add the peel and 1 maraschino cherry to the cocktail. Serve very chilled.

MAGNOLIA: Combine the white of 1 egg, juice of 1 lemon, 3 ounces Gin, ½ teaspoon grenadine, dash of heavy cream, and 3 to 4 ice cubes. Put in mixing glass, place a shaker on top of the mixing glass, and grasping them firmly together with both hands, shake vigorously 8 or 10 times. Remove the shaker, place a strainer on top, and pour into the well chilled glass.

VODKA

You can buy vodka from Russia, Poland, England, Austria, Holland, Finland, Denmark or America, made from potatoes or grain, flavored with orange, mint, grape, wild cherry, lime, or buffalo grass. A fifth will cost you anywhere from $3.79 for a domestic shot with a Russian-sounding name, to $8.53 for the Polish version called Polmos Zubrow-ka. That's the one with the blade of buffalo grass in it. This so-called bison herb, *zubrowka*, gives the colorless spirit a tinge of yellow and a bitterness only its fans truly admire. If it's ice cold, it's not so noticeable.

This is 1973. Twenty-eight years ago, in 1945, vodka was something Russians drank, which sold well only in Russian, Polish, or Ukrainian neighborhoods. In liquor stores you could find it on the back shelves with the cordials; vodka salesmen were trying to get it moved up into the "gin" section. The Morgan brothers, who were operating a very fine English restaurant on the Beverly Hills end of the Sunset Strip, called the Cock 'n Bull, introduced two drinks, with British overtones, like their short but splendid menu, the Pimm's Cup (with all its variations), and the Moscow Mule. This was 2 ounces of vodka, ice, ginger beer in a copper mug, with a quarter of a lime for garnish. It took. Vodka began to move.

Then someone linked it with a word: *"breathless."* You could, it suggested, take aboard several "martinis" made with it, and, all else being equal, return from a long lunch without leaving a distillery scent in your wake.

That did it. Vodka moved into the "gin" section all across the land. In most fashionable bars today, like the Cock 'n Bull, which is still doing business at the same old stand with its own built-in charisma, vodka outsells gin 3 to 1. The Oak Room at Hernando Courtright's Beverly Wilshire Hotel now features Henri's Oyster Bar at the entrance, tempting the trade from 5 to 7:30 p.m. with oysters bedded in ice nestling next to a very handsome crystal bottle of Masquer's English Vodka which is, you'll notice, 91.5 proof. Cold and neat, it's quite effective.

Right here, it's time to lay to rest some common misconceptions about vodka and Russia. It is *not* exclusively a potato spirit in the one-time land of the czars. *Some,* but not all Russian vodka is made from potatoes. The better vodka is made from grain, not only in Russia, but everywhere else. On excellent authority, we also have it that the vodka which Russian tosspots consume is *not* liquid dynamite; it is distributed at 80 proof. Taken neat, in small glasses, frequently, however, it can have bombing effects with the "one swallow" technique of Slavic tradition.

To approach an evaluation of vodka, it is first necessary to understand something of the nature of distilling. For this, not even page two of the sorcerer's book of alchemy is needed; it's even more elementary. The boiling point of water is 212°F. when it vaporizes, or turns to steam. The boiling point of alcohol is 176°F. So, if you apply heat to any batch of alcohol-containing mash, mush, malt, or wine, and keep the temperature below 212°F. you can separate the alcohol from the original fluid. It rises as steam through coils which, when cooled, cause condensation. That steam turns to liquid, and is the colorless spirit known as alcohol. *It is not yet a potable beverage.* To become any one of many variants of this order, refinements are required. The product will have character relating to its origins, as brandy comes from wine, rum from sugar cane, and whisky from grain. A totally pure spirit— 200 proof—or 100 percent alcohol, may be refined from any base. For beverage purposes, however, 190° proof spirits are good enough. These are known as *cologne spirits* or *neutral spirits.* They bite, and have little pleasing character. They have impurities, fusel oils, acids, aldehydes in relation to the material from which they were distilled. To become potable beverage, like vodka, there must be rectification. The spirits are filtered through charcoal, and that charcoal must be replaced on a regular schedule in relationship to the volume or quantity of spirits treated.

The United States Treasury Department, which is very concerned with collecting taxes on rectification of spirits, defines vodka quite clearly:

"Vodka *is neutral spirits distilled from any material at or above 190 proof, reduced to not more than 110 and not less than 80 proof and, after such reduction in proof, so treated . . . as to be without distinctive character, aroma or taste.*

The quality control of better vodka, you may now understand, relates to the integrity of the filtration through charcoal and, to some extent, upon the findings which have made those neutral spirits to begin with. Ben Dimsdale, the knowledgeable host of The Windsor Restaurant, in Los Angeles, states the quality platform which governs his award-winning career, as applicable to making vodka as well as operating a restaurant: "Buy the best and forget the rest." In his opinion, "potato spirits are putrid."

As we said at the beginning, you can buy the wildest variety of vodkas today. You can pay what you like—and some may taste like kerosene. The brand rosters read like a Russian telephone book! You'll come on some unlikely names, too, like Cooper, Newport, Canada Dry, Glenmore, and McCormick! That last one is an American vodka that comes 100 proof in a jug! Almost all the gin houses; Gordon's, Gilbey's, Hiram Walker's, Schenley's and Fleischmann's have their vodka stills going too. Smirnoff leads the parade in sales. Customers may not know their geography well enough to be able to locate the peninsula of Kamchatka, but even if that same customer comes in and asks for "Come catch me!" that's the vodka he'll get!

There's a reasonable flurry now in the market for English vodka, because so many folk drink it "on the rocks" where quality really shows up. Moving into this field is Borzoi English Vodka, from the solidly quality-built house of Kobrand. This vodka comes from James Burroughs, Ltd., of London who make Beefeater Gin. Soft, delicate, and clean! It's 91.5 proof—just right for the perfect Vodka Martini. Nuf sed! So, you can see, you don't have to go out and buy Stolichnaya Russian Vodka, or even Russkaya, two leading grain spirit vodkas from the Soviet Union, to know what a good or better vodka tastes like. If you *want* to taste a spud spirit, there's one called *Bolshoi*. Would you believe this potato-spirit vodka comes from France? It really does!

Earle MacAusland, the distinguished editor of *Gourmet Magazine* has said that a certain English vodka is the "preference of the discerning epicure." Certainly the quality is there. But there are excellent American vodkas, too, when it comes time to concoct your pet refresher, be it Vodka Martini, Gimlet, Bull Shot, Screwdriver or Bloody Mary. That you may have one truly reliable recipe, *from the source,* here's the way Lester and Sam Gruber make the *Bull Shot* at their superb London Chop House, in Detroit, where they invented this nutritious wonder!

The Bull Shot
(As served at the London Chop House)

Fill a double on-the-rocks glass with ice. Pour over it 1½ ounces of Vodka. Add a wedge of Lemon. Give it a gentle squeeze and drop it into the glass. Fill the glass with Campbell's Beef Bouillon (undiluted). Sprinkle with salt. Add a dash of Lea & Perrins Worcestershire Sauce, and garnish with 1 stick of celery as a stirrer.

The ways to go with vodka are as limitless as the ways of a man with a maid. These are some well-tested favorites:

VODKA GIMLET: Two ways to make this. Take juice of 1 fresh lime, add 1 teaspoon powdered sugar and 1½ ounces Vodka. Shake well with cracked ice and strain into 4 ounce cocktail glass. Or, take 4 parts Vodka and 1 part Rose's sweetened lime juice. Shake with cracked ice and strain into cocktail glass. I prefer the latter.

SCREWDRIVER: Put 2 or 3 cubes of ice into a 6 ounce glass. Add 2 ounces Vodka. Fill balance of glass with orange juice and stir. (A new twist: use Southern Comfort instead of Vodka.)

VODKA MARTINI: Chill 3-ounce cocktail glass to the point of frost. Fill Martini pitcher with cracked (not crushed) ice and pour in 1½ ounces Vodka. Then pour ½ ounce dry Vermouth. Stir briskly and strain at once into frosty glass. For those who prefer much "dryer" Martinis, change proportions to as much as 7 Vodka to 1 dry Vermouth.

BLOODY MARY: 2 jiggers tomato juice, 1 jigger Vodka, ½ jigger fresh lemon juice and a dash of Worcestershire sauce. Salt and pepper to taste. Shake with cracked ice and strain into 6 ounce glass.

VODKA STINGER: 1 ounce Vodka, 1 ounce white Creme de Menthe. Shake all ingredients well with cracked ice and strain into 3 ounce cocktail glass.

GYPSY COCKTAIL: Combine 1½ ounces Vodka with ¾ ounce Benedictine and a dash of bitters. Stir well with cracked ice and strain into 3 ounce cocktail glass.

HARVEY WALLBANGER: Follow directions for Screwdriver and float 1 oz. Galliano on top.

GRASSHOPPER COCKTAIL: Frothy and fresh. Combine ¾ ounce Vodka, ¾ ounce green Creme de Menthe and ¾ ounce white Creme de Cacao. Shake well with cracked ice and strain into 3 ounce cocktail glass.

MOSCOW MULE: An excellent tall drink in a beer mug or an 8-ounce glass. Place 2 or 3 ice cubes in the glass and add a dash of fresh lime juice and 3 ounces Vodka. Fill the mug with ginger beer (6 ounces), and top with 1 slice of lime.

VOLGA BOATMAN: Into a 4-ounce, chilled cocktail glass, combine juice of ½ orange, 3 ounces Vodka, 1 teaspoon kirsch and 3-4 ice cubes. Place a shaker on top of the glass and grasping them firmly together with both hands, shake vigorously. Remove the shaker, place the strainer on top of the mixing glass, and pour into the cocktail glass.

SPUTNIK: Combine 1 ounce Fernet-Branca, 2 ounces Vodka and ½ teaspoon superfine sugar in a mixing glass and stir with a bar spoon to dissolve the sugar. Add the juice of 1 teaspoon fresh lime or lemon juice and 3-4 ice cubes. Place a shaker on top of the mixing glass and grasping them firmly together with both hands, shake vigorously 8 or 10 times. Remove the shaker, place a strainer over the mixing glass, and pour into a chilled cocktail glass.

BLACK RUSSIAN: Combine 1 ounce Kahlua coffee liqueur and 3 ounces Vodka in a mixing glass. Add 2-3 ice cubes and stir gently. Place a strainer over the mixing glass and pour into a chilled 4-ounce cocktail glass.

The Tropical Grass you can Drink is Called

FROM SOMEWHERE SOUTH of Pango-Pango, in Sadie Thompson country, rum got its 20th century lift. The sultry lure of the tropics, palm-thatch, tapa cloth, prickly blow-fish, outrigger canoes, orchids and coral, fishnet and glass bubble-floats, all this and more decorative souvenir stuff from vagabondia of the South Pacific is synonymous with the haunting flavor of rum.

Before Don the Beachcomber set up his bar in Hollywood in the early 30's, with "monsoon rains" on the back bar by an outside garden hose, rum was a "Yo-ho-ho!" drink with a rich, but limited lore of pirates and English navy tradition. Trader Vic came along about the same time, in the San Francisco bay region, and with standing room only in Oakland, launched not only the Zombies and a bookfull of rum drinks, but a whole index of culinary succulence now known as "Polynesian Cookery." The tropical theme became more famous than Somerset Maugham's *Sadie Thompson*, and a "Missionary's Downfall" suggested only an original rum concoction by Don the Beachcomber! There's scarcely a village in the land today that doesn't have some kind of saloon with bamboo and palm-fronds offering rum drinks that taste good and look, sometimes, spectacular!

Rum is the only grass you can drink. It's made from a common reed called sugar cane—*saccharum officinarum*—and quite possibly a contraction of this Latin botanical name has given us "rum." In 18th century England, however, "rum" was a slang expression, the popular equivalent of today's "groovy." One British admiral's prescription for scurvy, in 1745, was to substitute the West Indian distillate of sugar cane for the sailor's small beer ration. The change, as you might imagine, was "rum" of the first order!

We may not know for sure where the name came from, but you can be sure today where your rum comes from by its name. All kinds of rum (there are hundreds of brands, but only three types) are made from sugar cane, the fermented juice of the reed, and the various by-products, which include molasses, and an odd scum called "dunder."

There's palm sugar, beet sugar, and cane sugar. Now, just how do you get either the sparkling crystals of sweetness, or pungent liquor from those basic botanicals? You begin with a cauldron, just like the witches' kettle in "Macbeth." Nectar from palm blossoms, crushed beets, or sugar cane juices are "like a hell-broth" brought to "boil and bubble." The scum that rises is called "dunder," into which yeast spores will settle and start a fermentation that gives part of Jamaican rum its peculiarly pungent taste. The sugar crystals are removed from the boiled-down syrup by a centrifuge, and the residual matter is molasses. Rum is the alcoholic distillate of the fermented juice of sugar cane, sugar cane syrup, sugar cane molasses, and/or with other sugar cane by-products, distilled at less than 190 proof, possibly reduced prior to bottling to not less than 80 proof.

From three types, many tastes. Rum, not unlike wine, reflects the country of its origin, and *each type of rum takes its name from its place of origin*, and is individually distinguished by its own flavor, body, and bouquet. The complex of rums in this way can baffle the customer, intrigue the bartender, and enrich the legends of each rum concoction! Recipes later. Here are the three types:

(1) *Light, dry rums:* Puerto Rico, Virgin Islands, Cuba, Barbados, the Philippine Islands, and Mexico (Habanero) all produce the light, dry rums made in column stills from a fermented mash of molasses and water, which has had the addition of cultured yeast and a dollop of left-over mash from a previous distillation. It is filtered, like vodka, through charcoal, and emerges clear and silvery. A small amount of caramel is added to give a uniform color. Lighter colored rums, called "Silver" or "White" or the language equivalents, describe the lightest rums. "Gold Label" or "Amber" describe deeper caramel-colored rums which are often older, with more pronounced flavor, and possibly a touch of sweetness. From Cuban rum, the Bacardi cocktail was born, with its alter-ego from Puerto Rico, the Daiquiri.

(2) *Rich, full-bodied rums:* Jamaica, Demerara, Martinique, New England, and London Dock Rum are those marvelously fragrant rums that really give the whole idea of rum its particular magic. These rums are made differently, in pot stills, with dunder and molasses, and age in oak puncheons. Some of the color derives from age in oak, but there's that dark mahogany richness from caramel. Myers's, the

"Planter's Punch" brand comes, like the label says, from Kingston, Jamaica, at 84 proof. It's a real groovy rum, or is that redundant?

Demerara rum takes its name from the Demerara River in British Guiana, South America, where sugar cane grows along the banks. The fascination of Demerara rum is its frequently high proof, for some brands peg it at 84, 96, 98, 114, and for the Zombie, 151 proof! Darker than Jamaican rums, but less pungent in aroma, they're lighter in taste because they're made in column, not pot, stills. Though he won't say so, there's probably some Demerara rum in Don the Beachcomber's Navy Grog (his original), because this high proof spirit has long tradition in cold northern waters as a bracer in raw weather.

Naturally, England is British Jamaica's best market. Rums shipped to England for aging and blending in bonded warehouses on the Thames are logically known as London Dock Rums.

New England rum is a tradition with centuries of trading between our young country and the islands of the West Indies. It was Columbus who brought sugar cane from the Canary Islands to the West Indies. Colonial traders exchanged manufactured goods for sugar and molasses, and the New England settlers did their own distilling.

(3) *Pungent, aromatic rums:* The paradise island of Java lends special qualities to the rum called *Arak*, produced from the Batavian sugar factories of modern Djakarta. But there are ages of traditional difference in the making of rum here. The molasses is treated with water that plunges down through the jungle. A wild yeast, *Saccharomycetes Vorderanni* and *Monilio Javanica* transform the mash. Little cakes of red Javanese rice are placed in the fermenting vats of watered molasses. The distilled Arak is then aged three or four years, then traditionally shipped to Holland for another period of aging, before blending and bottling. The end result is a rum of exceptional aromatic pungency, in a class by itself. It's the haunting stick in Swedish Punch. Swedish Punch? A liqueur blended in Sweden, with a rummy base.

Recipes? The secrets of Coca Cola belong to the parent company, and they're keeping them. The only way you can come close to Don the Beachcomber's Mai Tai is to buy the mix. An inside tip told me that the drink originated in Tahiti, where those two words mean "Number One" or " The Best!" and quite probably there's a kiss of the orchid bean called vanilla therein. If you want to taste the rum drink that

Frank Sinatra bought for Elizabeth Taylor at the Palm Springs Don the Beachcomber hideaway, ask for "The Cleopatra": creamy, smooth, and sweet for after dinner.

Trader Vic suggests that a whole tribe of little Hawaiian trolls called Menehunes help prepare his drinks. "Menehune Juice" is like a Mai Tai, with a double shot of Light Puerto Rican rum, fresh lime, orgeat, Mai Tai mix, and garnished with a pineapple finger, mint leaves, and a bright red cherry—and a Menehune!

To catch the inside flavor of professional Polynesian rum drinks suggests different rums on the back bar, a working familiarity with Falernum (an almond-flavored liquid from the West Indies) and orgeat, the thick almond-syrup. Whirring frozen Daiquiris in a blender might even catch you adding Lime Life-Savers. Hmm? The basic formula is simple:

DAIQUIRI: 2 ounces white rum; juice of ½ fresh lime; 1 teaspoon sugar. Shake well with cracked ice; strain into a chilled cocktail glass.

The variations are endless . . . and infinitely improved with a teaspoon of Jamaican floated on top. That's real rum perfume. The floating gardenia is for Sadie Thompson, should her ghost appear.

BACARDI: In a glass or shaker add cracked ice and these ingredients: 2 ounces light rum, 1 tablespoon lemon or lime juice, ½ teaspoon sugar and a dash of grenadine. Shake well and strain into chilled glass.

CUBA LIBRE: For that tall drink almost everyone seems to enjoy fill a Tom Collins glass with these good things: 3 ounces rum, juice of ½ lime, few ice cubes, cola drink to the top (about 6 ounces) and perch a lime slice on the rim.

MAI-TAI: This is a busy drink, simple to make and a taste which brings on smiles from guests.

> 2 ounces dark Jamaica rum
> ½ ounce apricot brandy
> ½ ounce curacao
> Juice of ½ lime
> 3-4 ice cubes

Combine the above in a glass or shaker and go to it with vigor. Strain into a cocktail glass and add a stick of fresh pineapple ½ inch wide and a few inches long.

Additional Recipes

Soft Fire of the Desert Lily...
TEQUILA

AFICIONADOS OF TEQUILA will tell you that the fiery distillate of the century plant ages in wood, like brandy, to become incredibly smooth. They should know. They drink it neat! In time-honored traditions of Mexico, the straight shot is an automatic ritual of quick dispatch. Salt goes on the web between the thumb and index finger of the left hand. A fresh-cut lime rests readily within reach. Begin! Drink the Tequila, lick the salt, suck the lime! The warm glow begins.

There's been no time to tell how smooth the Tequila might be, but unlike vodka, beyond the refinements of double distillation, the fermented "honey-water" of the handsome cactus plant has defining character.

The word "Tequila" derives from *Tuiquila*, the name of an Aztec tribe which inhabited the region of Jalisco near Guadalajara prior to the conquest and later gave its name to the town. There are written records of Tequila distillation as early as the 17th century, making this indigenous spirit the earliest *aqua vitae* of this continent. Apocryphal Aztec legends aside, the primitive process is interesting. The liquor is born from the heart of a species of cactus called *mezcal agave* or *mezcal maguey*. As an ornamental plant of the lily family, *genus amaryllis*, it is not unknown in California, where it is commonly called a "century plant" because it takes so long to bloom. The radiating corona of leaves, like a cluster of swords, is both formidable and handsome. Each blade is edged with a puncturing, scallop-pattern of needle-sharp thorns. The convex-concave surface reveals a subtle cameo design in gray-green variations. Fibers of these sturdy leaves will make native cloth when the hearts of the plants are harvested.

The moment of harvest, for cutting the "pineapple" out of the center of each plant, is from eight to twelve years in coming! As anyone knows, who's ever observed the time of blooming of a century plant, the flowering stalk shoots heavenward with an extraordinary thrust, and the leaves, which were so protectively vigorous, wither and fall in writhing ruin. The heart of the *mezcal agave* is cut out at just the moment of maturity when the rush of sap to the base of the plant occurs. It was a smart, patient Aztec that figured that one out.

According to one historian, a fire that swept over the region of Jalisco roasted the mezcal plants "which were much enjoyed by the natives." Apparently, the left-overs fermented after a drenching rain, and lo and behold, the liquid fire-of-the-gods trickled from the cactus!

Sophisticated modern distillation is not too far from these primitive principles. Where early Tequila-makers placed the pumpkin-size, sap-filled hearts of *mezcal agave* in fire-filled pits like a Texas barbecue, cooking them under a steamy cover of wet earth, today they are split open and steamed for eight hours, the *aguamiel* (honey water) sap running out freely. The fibrous "pineapple" is then shredded and all the remaining juice extracted mechanically. All the combined juice flows into large vats, for fermentation, which is started with a small batch of must from a previous fermentation. This insures a continuity of character.

After two or three days of fermentation, the fermented *aguamiel* is distilled in pot stills. The condensed vapors from these stills, when fresh, is called "tuba." It will rest for 15 days, and then be redistilled, to emerge at 104° proof as Tequila! "Silver" Tequila is reduced to the desired proof with distilled water, and bottled at once. "Gold" Tequila is aged in oak vats for at least four years.

All distillations of *mezcal agave* are not necessarily Tequila. Being a product of indigenous water and a native plant, subtle variations in the ultimate liquor are possible. Only that which is produced in the towns of Tequila, Arenal and Amatitlan, and in the area of Los Altos de Jalisco around the town of Arandas are authentic Tequilas. All Tequila is *mezcal*, but not all *mezcal* is Tequila. Allasamee—Cognac and brandy.

So, if you want to taste the real thing (and according to the records, 45,000,000 liters of mezcal are produced annually in Mexico, of which only 15,000,000 are legitimate Tequila), be selective. Jose Cuervo and Arandas Tequilas are both available in *Gold* at 86° proof, and *Silver* at 80° proof. Each of these is first rate, fine quality Tequila.

Moving towards that aged, soft, smooth Tequila of the *aficionado*, be on the look-out for Tequila Herradura (Horse Shoe Brand). It's distilled and bottled in Mexico, at 96° proof, costs more, has an aroma of tingling sunshine-swept grasses. It's too good for Margaritas. You can even get through the shot-glass, salt, and lime ritual in slow motion, enjoyably!

And now—the *Margarita!* Once you've experienced that version of this exquisitely refreshing cocktail as devised by Nichols clan of the La Paz restaurants of Laguna Beach, Orange, and Fullerton, California, no other Margarita is worthy of the name. It comes in a smoky crystal goblet, rimmed with coarse (kosher) salt crystals, creamy, cold, fragrant of fresh lime and lemon, tantalizing and satisfying, both sweet and sour, with a foamy, crushed ice head on it that lasts until you've drained the last drop and ordered another! Every bartender for miles around has tried to copy it. Sid Nichols tells me the secret is in using crushed ice in the blender, but he also admits they have a proportion of fresh egg white in their sweet-sour pre-mix formula that's made with *fresh* lemons and limes. The Jurgensen's Wine and Spirits Department at Fashion Square in Santa Ana has so many calls for the La Paz Margarita recipe, they commissioned spies to get the formula. Their findings, for a round of 4 drinks, are summarized with this version:

MARGARITAS CHAMPANEROS DE LA PAZ:

> 4 ounces Tequila
> 1½ ounces Triple Sec
> 1½ ounces Rock Candy Syrup
> ⅛ teaspoon Powdered Egg White

Combine all ingredients in a blender with crushed ice. Blend until thoroughly mixed and frothy. Pour into a stemmed wine goblet, the rim of which has been rubbed with the cut edge of fresh lime, and turned in a saucer of kosher salt.

When I showed the recipe to Sid Nichols, he just shook his head, and handed me a bottle of a new product called La Paz Margarita Mix. With that, all you need is the ice, the blender, Tequila and salt.

But the Magarita is not the only cocktail you can make with Tequila. Try a "Brave Bull": equal parts of Tequila and Kahlua over the rocks with a lemon twist. Or a "Charlie Goodlay" (that's a "Harvey Wallbanger") with orange juice, Galliano, and Tequila instead of Vodka.

Maurie Cooper, of Venice, California, who imports Tequila Herradura, has also been bringing *Sangrita de la Viuda* over the border from Guadalajara for gringos who appreciate good Tequila. It's a non-alcoholic mix which one Don Jose Sachez of Jalisco concocted almost fifty years ago. He had his own version of the Tequila quick-shot. He doused the fire with a bite into a cut orange sprinkled with chili powder and salt. Olé! It became the hallmark of his cantina at Lake Chapala. Then someone told Don Jose those two magic words—*"Bottle it!"* Today, his widow *(la viuda)* reigns over the ultimate product, called *"Sangrita de la Viuda."* The recipe has been modified to include tomato juice, with orange juice, and piquant seasonings. *No contiene alcohol,* senor; just add your own Tequila!

It's kind of sad to think that every time they cut the heart out of a *mezcal agave*, that noble eight-year-old cactus dies! But take comfort in knowing its use does not cease at once. The *aquamiel* that flows into the gaping hole quickly ferments, and in a few days, with a little added *madre pulque* (mother pulque), there's another national drink: *pulque!* It's more common than beer in Mexico, cheaper, and universally available. Good taste prevents me from any other description. Some say it suggests buttermilk, which I'd say is outrageously complimentary. *Pulque* is not for gringos; but Tequila, distilled from the heart of our most handsome indigenous cactus, is easily for everyone!

TEQUILA COLLINS: Same as for a Tom Collins except substitute Tequila for the Gin.

TEQUILA SOUR: Mix together 2 ounces Tequila, 1 teaspoon powdered sugar and juice of ½ lemon with cracked ice. Shake well and pour into a Sour glass. Fill with carbonated water and decorate with a cherry and half a slice of orange or lemon.

Additional Recipes

BRANDY VS COGNAC

A TASTE FOR COGNAC is a sometime thing; just plain brandy is often better.

Heresy? No, just plain unvarnished truth. Of all the brandies in the world, cognac is but one. It has a particular taste, for a particular clientele. In the United States, that clientele is a measured minority. Of the total brandy consumption in our country, imported brandies of all types, of which French Cognac is but one, account for only 25 per cent of the total. But before blood pressures rise among the connoisseur group, it must be admitted that a truly fine cognac is a splendid thing, of a noble history which links Napoleon and Churchill among its most passionate advocates. A small amount of a *Grande Fine Champagne Cognac* lying like a pool of molten gold in a thin crystal snifter, its "tears" running rivulets down the sides of the glass after a toying swirl of the warming palm, seems one of man's most luxurious indulgences. As the rare fumosity rises to penetrate the nostrils, an invisible fire tends to illuminate the mind, clearing the webs of thought to more concise articulation. Conversation becomes a grace of words and the moment of leisure is drawn from the well of time with singular opulence. *"He who aspires to be a hero must drink brandy,"* wrote James Boswell in his "Life of Dr. Johnson." Unquestionably it was French Brandy to which he was referring, and it was also French brandy which played the significant role in the classic anecdote told of Talleyrand, which suggests that drinking a fine Champagne brandy is only a small part of its enjoyment. Talking about it closes the circle of its experience.

It would be remarkable if there were not hundreds, even thousands, whose experience with this distilled spirit of wine, named for the Cognac district of its origin, did not parallel my own. My first encounter with the fiery liquid, which seemed only to sear my throat, left me in silent wonder about the extravagant praise rendered to cognac by some of my elders. I was just as sure their praise was as hypocritical among themselves as that of the courtiers whom the storybook tells us admired "the emperor's new cloak." Enjoying cognac was, if nothing else, *de rigueur*; and so I persisted, and from experience learned that reactions were quite possibly honest on some occasions, and frankly phoney when that good spirit had similar pretensions to undeserving grandeur. It requires courage or the folly of bad manners to suggest your host's Three Star libation is less than legendary! In droves, Americans have merely made their way to a more certain product of less controversial merit: fine California brandy, distilled, aged, and blended by master craftsmen, wherein the spirits rise as *"the soul of wine"* to become a clean, light bodied, mellow beverage which has no bite, burn, or roughness. The consumption of California brandy has doubled in the last ten years, and the figures are continuing in a dramatic rise. There is reason to the "why," and that's our story.

The art of distillation is almost as old as civilization itself. It was known to the ancient Egyptians. Centuries before Christ, the Chinese made spirits from rice wine. The word "alcohol" is Arabic in origin, and so is the "alembic" or the pot into which the source-wine would be placed for firing. It was probably an alchemist in the Dark Ages who discovered that alcohol vaporizes to become steam, at a lower temperature than water. The boiling point of water is 212°F., when it becomes steam, or vapor, and that of alcohol is 176°F. So, if heat is applied to wine, or other alcoholic liquid and the temperature is kept below 212°, all of the alcohol may be separated from the original liquid. The vapors are not allowed to escape into the air; they are wafted through coils in which they are condensed into liquid form again, emerging clear, colorless—distilled. If the material in the pot still has been a fine wine, the resulting alcohol, or "brandy" (deriving from archaic Dutch *Brandjwyn* for "burnt wine") carries the splendid essence of the grape along with it!

Proof? This is another archaic term still used to describe the measurable alcoholic strength of the distillate. To determine the potable strength of brandy, the English of olden days mixed it with equal amounts of gunpowder, then lighted it. If it failed to burn, it was too weak. If it burned too bright, it was too strong; but if the mixture burned with a bright and even blue flame, it was said to have been "proved." That potable mean today, we know was 50 per cent alcohol, by volume, which is 100 proof. Each degree of proof is equal to one-half of one percent alcohol. Ergo, a 90° proof beverage contains 45 per cent alcohol. The ideal for beverage brandy, and the standard for cognac, is 80°proof. Fine California brandies are also 80°. It is totally erroneous to believe that a 100° spirit is any better if it is "bottled in bond." That curious shibboleth of post-Prohibition whisky drinkers implied some kind of benign approval of the Federal Government. Nothing could be further from the truth. Uncle Sam's only interest in distilled spirits is the amount of tax he can collect on the alcohol as it flows from the still, into bond! But in brandy production today, Government *does* have one important function, even more discriminating than in the whisky field. Blending with neutral spirits, legal in the whisky business, is not permitted. Any California brandy is either a "straight brandy" or a "blend of straight brandies" and never a spirit blend. Flavoring agents are not permitted. Some European brandies, including cognac, obtain their taste characteristics from the most foreign essences: prunes, almond shells, and most often, Pedro Ximenez dark, sweet Sherry; and for coloring, caramel. Government labeling regulations further stipulate that no American brandy may be sold as such if it is not aged in wood for at least two years. For the better brandies, this is a minimum; for the cheapest, their maximum, accounting for some of the price differential in the market.

Further differences in the taste of brandy come from the type of still used. The old fashioned copper pot still produces brandy in slow, low temperatures, only 30 to 40 barrels per day. Pot still brandy brings a sunlight-clean taste, a bouquet from the grape reminiscent of a bunch of dried flowers, an elegance unobtainable from larger "continuous" stills. Continuous, vertical stills can produce 500 barrels of brandy per day, bringing a lightness needed for palatable blending.

The Government also provides the wary customer with a clue to the origin of the brandy in each bottle. The label must stipulate, as part of the printed legend, something of the spirit's pedigree. "*Made by*" does not necessarily mean, nor seldom indicate *distilling*, nor does "*Prepared by.*" These words indicate rectifying, which is composed of blending, filtering, aging, and bottling. The print is usually pretty small and misleading, but there's no mystery when it reads "*Distilled and Bottled by.*"

Christian Brothers, who crush their own grapes, make their own wine, and distill their own brandy, sell more brandy in this country than *all* imported brandies combined. Without waving a flag, or indulging in any chauvinistic prejudice, or even revealing any personal taste, it is possible to state flatly that these sales figures are as they are because the product is good, and preferred by that many customers. Why? Because the product was taste-engineered to the American palate. That particular technique has involved nothing more than using premium wines to begin with, pot still brandy aged in white oak, blended with continuous still brandies, all aged from 4 to 8 to 10 years, pre-blended into 200,000 gallon stainless steel tanks guaranteeing a dependable uniformity. Brandy at Christian Brothers is made only in the vintage harvest season, from September through November, when there is fresh free-run juice of grapes for winemaking. The slightest trace of sulphur on grapes will carry into wine through the still, becoming obnoxious in brandy. Christian Brothers' own vineyard grapes are sulphur-free. "Good brandy," in the words of Alfred Fromm, whose profound career with the grape forms substantial guiding counsel for the Christian Brothers, "must be made from new wine." Then follows that long, long aging in 50 gallon white oak barrels. Each barrel in itself represents extraordinary care by old-world trained coopers.

The blending marriage is accomplished with the artful judgment of experienced palates, to produce that clean, fruity taste, devoid of alien characteristics. How is this done? Brandy beyond 100° proof is too strong to taste without numbing the sensory apparatus almost instantly. Diluting with distilled water to 40° proof accentuates instantly the taste-nature of the product, its blessings of fruity origin, and any faults, or additives, as with European cognac and brandy. (For this reason, cognac-and-soda is seldom a good drink.)

Your own yardstick for determining quality in brandy is first and foremost your own taste preference. There are many Americans whose approach to brandy is via the cognac trail. This is a heavier taste, largely from pot still production and aging in Limousin oak, with possible additives adding further characteristics. Just for fun, dilute your favorite cognac with distilled water, to half-strength, then judge it by bouquet and taste. Compare it with your choice of California brandy. Almaden, Korbel, and Paul Masson brandies are three premium brands, blended and bottled by these houses to their own concepts of customer preference, and each has distinguished rosters of customer acceptance. Christian Brothers has walked away with the volume trade because it is never a sometime thing. It is without any pretension to the taste of cognac. It is proudly an American brandy for the American taste. It is not an imitation cognac; its own type has been accepted for what it is. It has all the universal use of brandy, as do the others, Almaden, Korbel, Paul Masson, for mixed drinks, (for wonderful Stingers) in snifters, and in the kitchen, lending flaming grandeur to chafing dishes in the dining room.

This is not a polemic against cognac. Cognac is the world's most famous brandy, but it is not always its best. It is sometimes the best, and on those occasions, the greatest! Initials and Napoleon's name on a bottle of French Cognac mean very, very little or almost nothing. Choose a distinguished trade name, then look for the little legend of origin. If it is a *Fine Champagne Cognac*, it's the best you can buy. It's quite possible, if your cognac is not so pedigreed, an American brandy will be better!

Wherever the grape grows and wine is made, in France, Germany, Spain, Portugal, Switzerland, Italy, Peru, Australia, South Africa, New York, or California, the soul of wine will be distilled, and aged to bring warming comfort. None will taste the same. Rejoice in their difference. Our California brandies have the certain touch of distilled magic and artful blending. None of them wear "the emperor's cloak."

STINGER: Add 2 ounces brandy (or cognac) and 1 ounce white crème de menthe to a glass with ice. Shake well and strain into chilled glass.

BRANDY ALEXANDER: Shake well, with ice 2 ounces brandy, 1 ounce each cream and crème de cacao. Strain into chilled cocktail glass.

BRANDY SOUR: Shake well with ice these ingredients: 2 ounces brandy, ½ ounce lemon juice, ¼ ounce orange juice, ½-1 teaspoon sugar. Strain into a chilled sour glass and place ½ lemon slice on side of glass.

BRANDY AND BITTER LEMON: Put a few ice cubes in a tall glass, pour 1½ ounces brandy over, add bitter lemon to taste and stir.

YUGENO: With Peruvian brandy, Pisco, this cocktail is a warming and healthy drink. In your bar shaker combine 1½ ounces fresh orange juice with 1½ ounces brandy and a few ice cubes. Shake, shake and shake some more! Pour into a chilled glass and inhale the fragrance before you sip.

FLIP: If you want to continue the fun of tasting wine after dinner, this is a must. For one cocktail, half fill that friendly shaker with cracked or crushed ice and add 1 teaspoon sugar, 2 ounces brandy (or port, sherry, rum) 1 egg, a dash of nutmeg and shake well. Strain into the electric blender and whirl for a few seconds.

THE BRANDY APPLE: An easy and warming drink for the fireplace on a wintry evening. Pour 2 ounces of brandy and hot apple juice in a coffee mug and sprinkle with a touch of cinnamon.

CALIFORNIA QUAKE: Don't be frightened by this one, but if it happens, you won't mind so much. In a large glass (about 10 ounces) shake 1½ ounces brandy, 1 ounce fresh lemon juice, 1 teaspoon sugar, together with some cracked ice. Strain into a cocktail glass and slowly fill with champagne! You may add an ice cube or two if desired.

SIDECAR: The proportions in this popular and easy-to-make drink may be varied according to your taste. Mix together ¾ ounce each brandy, Cointreau (or Curacao or Triple Sec) and lemon juice. Shake well with ice and strain into a glass already chilled.

Sweetness and Lightning! The World of
LIQUEURS

THERE IS A SCHOOL OF THOUGHT that insists no one can tell the difference between wine and water with his eyes closed and a clothes-pin on his nose. The taster will only, they opine, experience "wet." In strict theory, they *may* have an option on partial truth. The tongue relates touch and mouth-feel, and that great laboratory known as the "palate" depends in depth upon the chimney chasms rising from the mouth to the nose. For the wine-taster, this is the all-important distinction between *bouquet*, being the fragrance detected by the nose alone, and *aroma*, that subtle and complex, breathy after-effect in which the residual impression summons hopefully the grape-origins of the wine.

None of us, smokers included, are as bereft of our whole sensory apparatus as the man with a clothes-pin on his nose, but our *eyes* can play tricks upon tasting psychology.

For almost 800 years a Trappist Order of Cistercian monks has been making an exquisite liqueur from an ancient recipe developed by Frère Jean utilizing from 30 to 40 herbs, spices, peels, blossoms, and barks. This *Liqueur Monastique* is called *Aiguebelle*, and is produced in both green and yellow versions, like the Carthusian order's liqueur, Chartreuse. The brilliant emerald-green comes from plants, and almost shouts "Mint"! But it isn't mint at all, even though the eye-information keeps insisting. Eyes closed, nose open, you'll taste more than "wet"; a whole rush of different stimulae will crowd in for identification. None will be more than fleetingly insistent, and even heightened in simplicity over ice, will not betray the secret formula married in the maceration responsible for this elegant elixir compounded with fruit distillates, and aged in oak.

Liqueurs, often referred to as "cordials," and frequently confused with brandy, have a long history. We know that Hippocrates blended herbs and aromatic plants with wines, and so did the ancient Chinese. French historians credit Arnaud de Villeneuve with the discovery of *eaux-de-vie*, the distillate of fermented fruit. In the belief that this fiery strong spirit could be soothing to the nerves, when infused with herbs, he added macerations of sage and rosemary. The 12th century saw the flourishing growth of religious orders in France and Italy. They became wealthy centers of learning, rising in architectural splendor from surrounding vineyards and fields. They produced wines, and all kinds of herbal brews, and came to an understanding of distillation. With the Revolution in the 18th century, the vast church holdings were secularized, but those cherished formulas were never lost. Like the secret formula of Drambuie, from the Highland moors of of Scotland, which came to the Mackinnon family from Prince Charles Edward Stuart, the recipe for the elixir was a true treasure.

The secret of the finest liqueurs arises from its essential flavor, its perfume, the balance of sweetness and strength, all in a smooth enticing marriage, not unmindful of an exciting color, be it lemon yellow, gold, orange, red, purple, blue, green, or crystal clear flecked with gold leaf. The warming spirit, which slips down the throat like a caressing flame, may have several origins. That alcoholic source may come from neutral spirits, grain spirits, whiskey, rum, grape brandy, fruit spirits, or even rice alcohol. The quality comes from the nature of the base materials, the type of distillation, and the degree of rectification or re-distillation to remove impurities. The individual flavors of liqueurs are born of compounds of complicated chemical structures called essential oils. Many, taken alone, are downright disagreeable, but diluted in minute quantities, impart taste-effects of ethereal, transporting wonder!

Essential oils are extracted by pressure, maceration, percolation, or compounding with solvent liquids, even fats. The final compounding operation then requires maturing, filtration, and reduction to the proper proof with pure spring water before bottling.

There are literally thousands of liqueurs, but we can group them under six classifications. The alcoholic strength gives them long life, impervious to casual treatment. They keep, even after opening, so you may stock your bar plentifully without worry. The whole ceremony of service, in exquisite thin glass, or cut crystal provides a luxurious close to dining, and with some of the more exotic examples, rare adventure in taste.

How many of these do you know?

HERB LIQUEURS: *Aiguebelle:* a 12th century recipe, still produced at the same Trappist monastery in the Rhone Valley, subtle, velvet-smooth, jewel-hued green or yellow; *Benedictine:* first produced by Benedictine monks at Fecamp Abbey in 1510 to revive monastic fatigue, and combat disease, praised by Francis I, King of France, "Deo Optimo Maximo" (D.O.M.). Imitated, but never truly copied, it has no peer; *Chartreuse:* inexplicably, the Carthusian monks were expelled from France in 1903, and took their recipe for the smooth green and yellow liqueurs they'd been making for 900 years, to Tarragona, where they stayed until 1931. The green Chartreuse is 96° proof, the yellow 75° but both have enticing taste; *Cordial-Medoc:* this sweet red liqueur is as the name suggests, based on a concentration of French Claret, plus a marriage with extracts of herbs; *Drambuie:* the famed liqueur of Bonnie Prince Charlie, compounded with Scotch, honey, and secret herbs. Spiked with more Scotch makes the "Rusty Nail" of undeniable after-dinner appeal to the Scotch-drinker; *Fior d'Alpi:* Flower of the Alps, with crystals of sugar clinging to a branch in tall flute bottles, sweet, golden, complex; *Galliano:* named after Major Giuseppe Galliano who achieved a salutory victory in Abyssinia in the 19th century, but famed today for the "Harvey Wallbanger" cocktail blend of this unique liqueur with orange juice and vodka; *Irish Mist:* Irish whiskey, herbs, and honey in an excellent melange; *Izarra:* an Armagnac brandy base, flavored with herbs from the French Pyrenees; *La Vieille Cure:* half-a-hundred herbs steeped in Cognac according to a formula from an Abbey in the Gironde district of France; *Strega:* a golden yellow Italian liqueur with its own magic. *Strega* means "Witch," and this brew is said to unite forever two people who taste this elixir together; *Tuaca:* an Italian liqueur which resists definition, each sip beckoning another challenge.

CITRUS LIQUEURS—*Aurum:* made in the Abruzzi mountains of Italy, aged brandy pungent with orange peel and herbs; *Cointreau:* a French masterpiece of crystal clear triple-distillation from *curacao,* orange peel, made first by Edouard and Adolphe Cointreau in the early 19th century. Cooking with Cointreau, too, is not be overlooked. (Try a "Rolls Royce Cocktail," equal parts of Cognac, Cointreau, and orange juice, shaken with ice!) Crème *de Mandarine:* presenting the subtle essential oil of the tangerine in a delightful liqueur; *Curacao:*

originally a distillate of dried orange peel from the West Indian Island of Curacao, but now a generic term for orange liqueur. The triple-stage rectification process, making the water-white liqueur gave rise to the alternate name, *Triple Sec; Parfait Amour:* usually violet-colored, scented like Crème *de Violettes*, it is basically a citrus-flavored exotic liqueur; *Van Der Hum:* from South Africa, flavored with indigenous fruits, herbs, seeds, and bark, created by Dutch settlers yearning for their remembered Curacao. The name is a pun for "What's his name ...," no one could recall the inventor.

FRUIT LIQUEURS—*Apricot Liqueur:* From France comes Abricotine, Apry, and from Holland, Apricot Brandy, made from macerated ripe fruit, crushed kernel extracts, and grape brandy. "Brandy" in connection with apricot is a misnomer. A true "apricot brandy" is clear white, dry *eaux-de-vie; Blackberry Liqueur:* deep purple, from ripe fruit and brandy; *Blackcurrant Liqueur;* Crème *de Cassis:* the finest comes from Dijon, where it has been made since the 16th century, and today helps make the fashionable *Kir*, being dry white wine, over ice, in a tumbler-highball, but in strictly spoonful amounts; *Creme de Fraises* (strawberries); *Fraises de Bois* (wild strawberries); *Bananes* (bananas); *Peach; Framboises* (raspberries); *Prunelle* (plum), the ripe fruit in brandy, sweetened; *Cherry Heering:* made first by Peter Heering in a small shop in Denmark 150 years ago, a superb cherry brandy; *Maraschino:* water-white, highly perfumed distillation of fermented maraschino cherries and their crushed pits, a Venetian invention, invaluable to the connoisseur dessert chef; *Southern Comfort:* mellow Bourbon whiskey infused with the added elegance of ripe peaches, and a hint of orange. Superb taken neat, or in dozens of cocktail concoctions; *Sabra:* an exotic from Israel, red, bitter-sweet, handsomely packaged, made from an indigenous cactus, chocolate, and orange.

FROM BLOSSOMS AND LEAVES, NUTS, BEANS, AND KERNELS, ETC.—*Cherry Blossom Liqueur:* naturally, from Japan, by the distinguished Suntory distillery; Crème *de Roses:* from France, an elixir of rose petals; Crème *de Violettes:* Crème Yvette, named for French actress Yvette Gilbert, is the most famous, from Jacquin, naturally from the petals of violets; *Green Tea Liqueur:* haunting and beautiful, made from powdered tea and brandy, presented in ceramic bottles; Crème *de Cacao:* the popular Chocolate liqueur from cacao beans, available in rich brown or colorless, and today with variations like *Chococo* with Coconut, some with solid bits of chocolate, some with mint: Crème *de Café:* many variations descend from the spirit extracts of coffee: *Kahlua*, from Mexico, answering delectably the universal coffee taste-appeal, makes the "Black Russian," with vodka; *Tia Maria*, with a Jamaican rum base, plus spices; Crème *de Noyeaux*, from the penetrating perfume of peach and apricot kernels, a flavor-essence lift for the inventive bartender.

SINGLE HERB OR SPICE LIQUEURS—*Absinthe* (Pernod): an anything but ordinary opalescent liqueur invented in Switzerland by the French Dr. Ordinaire sent habituées of those 18th century days into limbo. The "Green Muse" as it was called, hooked the bistro sippers through the insidious aromatic leaves, not flowers, of wormwood. The recipe was sold in 1797 to Henri-Louis Pernod, whose name has been synonymous with the product since that time. Sale was prohibited in France and Switzerland before World War I, so Pernod manufacture was moved to Tarragona, Spain. Wormwood Absinthe is still banned in most countries, but the yellow-green anise-flavored Pernod, minus the pernicious leaf, still claims fans who affectedly render the liqueur milky by trickling drops of water into it through a lump of sugar perched on a silver spoon; *Anisette* and *Anis Del Mono:* water-white liqueurs of pure spirit from France and Spain, from aniseed, more delightful spooned over fresh peaches than to sip; *Ouzo:* is a drier, but equally aniseed liqueur, made milky white with water, of Grecian origins; Crème *de Menthe:* the blessed digestive garden mint was immortalized in liqueur first by the French. Get Frères *Pippermint* is one classic, Cusenier's *Freezomint*, another, and the Stinger Cocktail, made with brandy and the white mint version, a real knockout! Try one tipped with Pernod!; *Danzig Goldwasser* and *Kummel:* both carry the aromatic message of caraway, but the latter is flavor-tilted with anise, is flecked with bits of gold leaf, a hang-over from the medieval notion that gold was curative of many diseases; *Sambuco:* crystal clear Italian liqueur with a curiously fresh herb and licorice bite. *Eaux-de-Vie:* the true "Waters of Life" distilled from macerated, fermented stone fruit, usually dry, white, or relatively high proof. *Mirabelle* and *Slivovitz* are distilled from plums, and *Kirschwasser* from cherries, the latter imparting elegance of flavor to fruit compotes; *Calvados:* from Normandy's apple orchards is pot-distilled, aged golden in oak. Its close cousin is the American *Applejack.*

And for Christmas and holiday sipping, *Advocaat:* from Holland, thick enough to eat with a spoon, creamy, rich, golden yellow from dozens of egg yolks, plus brandy.

Our inventory has left out *Greek Metaxa* and *Batavian Arrac,* and *Amaretto* from apricot pits. There are fans for *Amer-Picon,* but bitters and brandy belong in other categories. The world of liqueurs is sweetness and lightning!

For a rainy night's diversion, with a warm fire crackling on the hearth, when all is quiet, have a go at building a *Pousse Café,* multi-layered. It can stack and build, as tremulous as a house of cards, but beautiful! Begin with that tall, tapering, thin glass, and an assortment of different colored liqueurs—once you've mastered the art—you'll be the envy of all those be-dazzled on party nights.

POUSSE CAFÉ: This 'rainbow cordial' is a brightly colored and strong tasting drink for after dinner. It requires a very steady hand and patience to have it look right. Start with a tall, thin, cordial glass on a flat surface. From 2 to 7 or 8 liqueurs may be used, but begin with the heaviest so that the liqueurs will not become scrambled. You will need a modified straw-and-funnel or a demitasse spoon upside down to pour over so as not to mix the liqueurs. Here we go! Slowly pour the following: ¼ ounce (or 1½ teaspoon) each . . . green crème de menthe, yellow Chartreuse, Cherry Heering and cognac. Other variations include: crème d'amande, white crème de menthe, Grand Marnier, Parfait amour and Crème Yvette. Have a camera ready the first time you try this and then settle back for some slow drinking.

Following are the weights of liqueurs and brandies that may be used in a pousse café. Be certain to use liqueurs with at least a point difference in weight in order to keep the layers separate.

Sloe Gin (66 Proof)	4.7
Kummel (82 Proof)	4.8
Peppermint Liqueur (60 Proof)	5.4
Peach Liqueur (60 Proof)	5.7
Rock & Rye Liqueur (70 Proof)	6.6
Liqueur Monastique (86 Proof)	7.4

Triple Sec (78 Proof) 7.9
Ginger Flavored Brandy (70 Proof) 8.0
Apricot Flavored Brandy (70 Proof) 8.1
Cherry Flavored Brandy (70 Proof) 8.4
Blackberry Flavored Brandy (70 Proof) 8.5
Peach Flavored Brandy (70 Proof) 8.7
Dry Orange Curacao (64 Proof) 10.4
Blackberry Liqueur (64 Proof) 11.5
Blue Curacao (64 Proof) 11.9
Cherry Liqueur (48 Proof) 12.0
Coffee Liqueur (60 Proof) 13.9
Apricot Liqueur (60 Proof) 12.7
Maraschino Liqueur (60 Proof) 14.3
Crème de Cacao, White (54 Proof) 15.1
Crème de Cacao, Brown (64 Proof) 15.2
Gold Liqueur (60 Proof) 15.2
Parfait Amour (58 Proof) 15.5
Crème de Menthe, Green, White or Gold (60 Proof) 16.2
Crème de Noyaux (60 Proof) 17.0
Anisette Liqueur, Red or White (50 Proof) 17.2
Crème de Banana (56 Proof) 18.2

ANGEL'S DREAM *(or Alfonso)*: An after-dinner delight to warm the insides. Pour 1½ ounces crème de cacao into a liqueur glass. Slowly slide about 3 dashes of heavy cream into the glass; a demitasse spoon usually works best. The cream should just float on the surface. For an

ANGEL'S KISS add a cherry on a toothpick and lay it across the glass.

GRASSHOPPER: Combine the following over 3 or 4 ice cubes in a mixing glass: 1½ ounces crème de cacao, 2½ ounces green crème de menthe and ½ ounce (1 tablespoon) heavy cream The mixing arm needs to work vigorously for nearly a dozen shakes, then pour this lovely brew into a chilled cocktail glass.

PIMM'S CUP NO. 1: This kooky international drink is bound to delight the taste buds. Combine the juice of one lime and 1 teaspoon superfine sugar in a Tom Collins glass and stir to dissolve the sugar. Add 2 or 3 ice cubes and 3 ounces Pimm's Cup No. 1 (a ginger based liqueur) with 1 lemon slice. Stand two strips of cucumber peel upright in the glass and fill with club soda or lemon if you prefer. A sprig of fresh mint is always in order.

TOMATE: Use one of those special tall wine glasses you have been saving. Place 2 ice cubes in the bottom and pour 4 ounces Pernod and 1½ teaspoons genadine; stir. Add 2 to 3 ounces of cold water and stir again.

AMERICAN BEAUTY: Pour each of the following into a cocktail shaker: ½ ounce each orange juice, Grenadine, dry vermouth, brandy and ¼ teaspoon crème de menthe. Shake well with cracked ice and strain into a chilled cocktail glass. If you have a fine port wine, a few drops on the top will add a special flavor.

METAXA

NEAT: Just as it is, in a jigger, or small cocktail glass.

THE GOLDEN GREEK: On-the-rocks with a lemon twist.

ALEXANDER, THE MANHATTAN, THE SOUR, THE FIZZ, THE SIDE CAR, THE OLD FASHIONED, THE STINGER . . . JUST SUBSTITUTE "METAXA."

THE DEVIL: Jigger White Crème de Menthe, and jigger Metaxa combined with ice. Shake until chilled. Pour into a cocktail glass and sprinkle with finely ground red pepper!

THE QUEEN'S PICK: Into a large wine glass pour an ounce of Metaxa over an ice cube or two. Fill the glass with champagne and find a comfortable chair.

COINTREAU

Try this versatile liqueur after dinner in a large wine bowl-type glass or on the rocks.

THE LONG GLEN: Mix 1 ounce Cointreau with 1 ounce gin and pour over ice in a highball glass. A touch of bitter lemon is good.

WHITE LADY: Measure 1 ounce Cointreau with 1 ounce each gin (or vodka) and lemon juice. Give a few good shakes with some cracked ice and strain into a glass.

BASIN STREET: Combine 1 ounce Cointreau, 1 ounce fresh lemon juice, 2 ounces bourbon with cracked ice. Shake well and strain into a cocktail glass.

CRÈME de KIRSCH

ROSE COCKTAIL: In a mixing glass add some ice and 1 pony Kirsch, 1 pony dry vermouth and a dash of grenadine. Shake well and strain into a chilled cocktail glass and drop a cherry on top.

ORANGE-KIRSCH COCKTAIL: If you forgot to take your Vitamin C this will help some of the MDR. In an old fashioned glass stir together 1 jigger Kirsch, 2 jiggers fresh orange juice and a dash of Anisette.

Additional Recipes

Index